REFRESHMENT IN THE DESERT

SPIRITUAL CONNECTIONS IN DAILY LIFE

GILBERT PADILLA

TWENTY-THIRD PUBLICATIONS
Mystic, Connecticut

Twenty-Third Publications
P.O. Box 180
Mystic, CT 06355
(203) 536-2611

Library of Congress Catalog Card Number 85-50663
ISBN 0-89622-228-4

Cover photos by William Haffey
Cover design by George Herrick
Edited by Eleanor Buehrig
Designed by Helen Coleman

In Memory of
Helen

Preface

"With all his ideas, Father Padilla should write a book." These words were said one Sunday morning after Mass by parishioner Linda Bednarik to Sister Helen at St. Ambrose Church in Tucson.

When Helen told me of this conversation, I was pleased and honored that a parishioner would think my ideas worth putting down. Since then many things have happened. Sister Helen died of cancer. A crushing experience of the Dark Night of the Soul entered my own life. Challenges of running a large city parish by myself introduced sorrows I had never dreamed of. The lives and sufferings of persons I dealt with seemed to parallel mine, something that I would have thought impossible before Vatican II. These circumstances and others recalled the suggestion of Linda and the encouragement of Helen.

The purpose of this book is to provide reading – while riding on the subway, during rest after lunch, or a short thought before turning out the light at bedtime. It provides meditation for the ordinary person looking for the connections of life. Some of the chapter titles may appear lofty, but they reflect our lives. I would hope that readers will discover how their lives are woven into these pages.

My thanks are offered to Sister Rosanna Gleason of the Sinsinawa Dominicans who painstakingly and prayerfully reviewed the expressions and thoughts in this book.

Contents

Introduction

O n the wall of the Picture Rocks Retreat House in Tucson, Arizona, are the words, "The desert will lead you to your heart, and there I will speak." These beautiful words from the book of the prophet Hosea remind us that we must retreat from the noise and activity of the city and go into the desert. There, in the silence of the depths of our hearts, God will speak to us. We will hear God in this stillness. Only in stillness and quiet do we truly hear him. Otherwise, all we hear is ourselves talking to ourselves and that is shallow conversation. This "going apart" is important these days when the tendency in religious expression seems to be noise, hustle, planning, doing, and moving. In this environment we are never still, quiet, or listening.

Hosea tells us that in the desert we will pray. What is prayer? Prayer is listening to God. Prayer is shutting down our self and listening to what he has to tell us. Prayer is contemplative silence. There are those who take offense at the thought of prayer as silent reflection. Still waters run deep: the deeper the waters, the more silent and still those waters are. This is not well accepted by those whose prayer life is surface noise and gymnastics. The invitation to the desert is to those who are never silent because they have so much to do.

But why the desert? What is so special about the desert? Those who have lived in the Southwest all our lives have no problem with the desert concept. There might be some concrete poured over it; yet, it is the desert. Our front and backyards are desert. Desert is around us and it is beautiful. I like to think that this reality is to our advantage.

The Israelites and Moses spent forty years wandering in the desert before they reached the Promised Land. Jesus spent forty days and forty nights in the desert before beginning his public ministry. After his conversion Apostle Paul went off to the Arabian desert for three years to pray and study. Unique about the desert is its profound spiritual quality that offers opportunity for peace and reflection.

At first glance the desert is harsh—foreboding and uninviting, barren and challenging, lonely. When we look at the desert and compare it with life in the city, then we begin to see what the desert is. The desert speaks to us and calls attention to its stark beauty. The dirt, the sand of different colors, the hard rocks—some jagged, some smooth—are distinctive elements of this raw beauty. We notice the small vegetation growing between the rocks and within the rocks themselves. There are cacti and tough mesquite shrubs that can live and thrive on rocky soil with very little moisture. The desert has its own sounds. The quieter and more open we become, the clearer we hear the sounds of nature in the desert around us. It is like the Simon and Garfunkel song, "Sounds of Silence." Silent sounds are there and they are beautiful. Now the dirt, rocks, cacti, shrubs, and sounds take on new aspects in the ways we see them. The desert becomes the center of silent activity of the untrammeled creation of God.

We will neither see this beauty nor hear it unless we allow the desert to speak to us. We must learn reverence and acceptance of God's creation. The cactus flower is not the tulip. If we expect it to be the tulip, we will never capture its beauty. The stark, rocky terrain of the dessert makes no claim to be anything but itself. If we do not accept creation as it is, then we destroy its beauty. When we accept the desert and its beauty, we accept ourselves and our own beauty. With this attitude, we take a step toward accepting others and their beauty. This step should slow us down and help us come to the place in our own heart where God will speak to us.

Jesus often went to the desert where he was absorbed in prayer. He told his apostles as he tells us, "Come off to a deserted place and rest awhile." In our own desert times we will know the gift and grace of that invitation.

1
Watch Out
For That Virtue

A young man runs to Jesus, does him homage, and asks, "Good Teacher, what must I do to possess eternal life?"
Jesus answers him with a question, "Why do you call me good? Only God is good." (This means, "Are you interested in what I have to say or are you trying to butter me up?") Jesus goes on, "You know the commandments." The man answers, "I have kept them all from the time of my youth."

Jesus looks upon him with love. Jesus likes this man. Did Jesus *like* some persons more than others? Did he *love* some more than he did others? Yes, he did. Here is one instance. As he sees the man's sincerity and zeal, he knows it is time to spring the greatest teaching of renunciation on him. Jesus tells him, "Go sell what you have and give to the poor and then come follow me. Then you will have riches in heaven." The young man goes away, for he has many possessions.

What a powerful lesson. It is twofold. The first lesson is that the man is sincere and virtuous; the second he's kept the commandments all his life. But he is relying on his virtue. He is proud of his virtue – proud of his goodness. Still

4

he wants to do the best. You might say that his response to Jesus' command is a challenge to Jesus. This is the young man's first mistake. No one should take a life of virtue and piety and hold it up to God for it to be noticed.

God will not be outdone in generosity. When Jesus offers the man treasure in heaven in exchange for the earthly treasures he must give up, the young man reveals his real lack of faith and courage. He would not relinquish his many possessions. (It has been said that one sign of our lack of faith in the resurrection and life eternal is greed in our world.) The man walked away sadly. He was sad because he really wanted what he asked for, but he could not make the sacrifice Jesus asked of him.

Walking away was the greatest mistake. When God asks something of us, who is able to do it on his own? No one. Remember, this young man had relied on his practice of virtue over the years, and if we rely on our own goodness, we are certain to come to a painful crash just as did the young man. Judas made a similar mistake. He did not ask Jesus for forgiveness. Forgiveness was there—he had but to ask for it. Similarly our young man had the answer in his grasp and let it go. He could have told Jesus, "I like what I hear and want to obey, but I find myself so attached to my money and possessions, that I can't give them up. I can't do it on my own but I know that you can do it for me and in me. You can effect in me what you ask of me." It could have been simple, but not easy. God never asks easy things of us. When the young man asked Jesus what he must do, and was given the answer, he did not follow through. He blew his chance.

There are some things that are in and of themselves divine—like forgiveness which is not within the human condition to produce. Here is where we have to question earnestly and sincerely. As individuals, who can forgive on his own? Yet, God asks this and other things of us. On our own we are headed for a collapse. It is only in realizing that we cannot forgive on our own that we can open ourselves to God to allow Him to work it out in us. Like the young man in the Gospel, let us beware of relying on our own virtue. In a second, God can show us how shallow this can be. There is only one hope. That is God and his mercy. And it is a grace to ask for the very grace of allowing him to work in us.

2

The Will of God

*P*eople who speak much about the will of God and doing God's will and doing things "His" way frighten me. So often I have heard this as another way of saying, "I accept your hard luck and your misfortune." I have seen individuals walk away from disasters they may have caused, leaving others to suffer, and then say, "Can't you see, it's God's will." Also, the advocates of God's will can secretly mean, "So long as things go the way I want them, it is God's will." One definition of an optimist is one who tells you to buck up when things are going his way. It is much the same with the "will-of-God" flag-waver. The hardest thing we have to learn in life is to allow those we love to suffer. People who harp on the will of God seem to have learned that lesson too well. The will of God means that we look inward and at our own sufferings. It is not telling others, "That is your problem." In no way can the will of God be construed as causing pain and grief to others as we get off scot-free.

And the will of God is not crystal ball gazing to make sure we do right. It is not asking for a sign either. This ritual of praying, "O God give me wisdom so that I will make the right decision," is all right provided it is not just another way of saying, "Please God, don't let me mess this up and suffer a humiliation or a failure or anything like that." The will of God is not to behave in such a way that we escape all suffering. That is nothing more than trying to manipulate God's will so that it becomes our will. We are not going to go through life without making a mistake and causing suffering to ourselves and to others. In fact, even without making these mistakes, we will cause enough suffering all around. This cannot be avoided.

But Solomon had a marvelous idea when he asked for wisdom to rule wisely. This did not mean that all his decisions brought happiness to everyone. The correct decision at times will cause severe unhappiness. The woman who has two men in love with her is an example. This is the eternal triangle. She must make a decision. She does not want to hurt anyone. But no matter what decision she makes, right or wrong, someone is going to be hurt. It would be a consolation to be certain when making correct decisions—about personnel, policy, purchases, and squabbles among people. But even with correct decisions there is no assurance that some would not suffer. The will of God, then, cannot be looked upon as a way of doing the right thing and taking the correct next step so that all will be a bed of roses.

The will of God is not really future. It is in a sense more in our past. It means that we look back on the failures, disappointments, and crushing humiliations; the successes and the triumphs and all of life, and that we look upon happenings without anger, bitterness, resentment, or rancor. When we accept the will of God, we see where we have been and see that much of what we had planned and worked for and desired never came to be the way we wanted. When we make too many plans and strive too hard for anything, many times we produce disaster. The will of God means that we accept our great hurts gracefully as truly his way of working in us.

"I am still grieving over this, and this hurt I will carry with me to the grave, yet I know that it just had to be God's will for me. He wills the best for me and this sorrow that

I must bear now and will bear for a long time to come is for my greater good. He knows, even though I don't, and even though I still agonize, I accept it willingly because it is his will for me.

3

The Delegated Parish
O Grief!

*T*he pre-Vatican II parish was similar to St. Dominic Parish in the movie, *Going My Way.* The pastor was in the mold of Father Fitzgibbons. The associates (called assistants in those days) were like Bing Crosby who did little pastoral work. The church and parish were stereotyped in the media to the "nth" degree.

Primarily, the pastor was chief custodian of the parish plant. Every day he would count the number of buildings he was responsible for. He would check to see if all the classrooms of the school were still there and if all the employees had come to work on time. All roads led to the rectory. All problems within the parish could, and had to be, handled there. No priest should ever go to a parishioner's home except for a sick call. An assistant could leave the rectory to make the bank deposit, teach his class in the school, and visit the hospital. Then he quickly returned to the warmth and protection of the rectory to keep himself "unspotted from the world." "Back at the ranch," he could be on duty and write his sermon.

In those days, the rectory was the citadel of stagnation. It was unheard of that a priest be present at an inquest or at a union meeting. Those events were off limits. His job was to be present and available at the rectory. This created an abyss between clergy and people. Lay people had their role in the life of the church. Pray, pay, and obey. Parish life was a giant housekeeping affair. The pastor made all the decisions and the utmost spiritual endeavor was the annual parish mission – usually a theological disaster.

Socially, the parish consisted of the Men's Club, the Ladies' Sodality, the PTA, the CYO, the Legion of Mary, and the St. Vincent de Paul Society. All of these were valued and to be praised. Except for the latter two organizations, they were spiritually sterile. I read of a man who left the church to become a Jehovah's Witness so that he could do something apostolic. He observed that the main activity of the Men's Club of the parish was to review the films of the last Notre Dame football game. (That had to be when Notre Dame was winning their games!) The choir dinner, the parish picnic, and the bazaar were musts of activity for the priests.

The attitude of the priests in pre-Vatican II days was something else. A priest ordained into the diocesan priesthood looked ahead to the time when he would be pastor. He counted those ahead of him in seniority. The topic of conversation among the priests focused on internal politics of the church. Questions were always part of clerical gatherings: Does the bishop like you? Who will get the assignment to St. Something Parish? Which assistant will go to Father X? On their day off to play golf, priests got together and discussed diocesan policies or their upcoming vacations. When a priest was appointed pastor, this was tantamount to a coronation – he had made it and could settle in for the rest of his life. The pastor was very much "involved" since every minute decision was referred to him. The sense of power and authority was overwhelming. Many times, he meddled with authority. He could, of course, "go up" from his first pastorate and he should expect to be promoted. The mentality of the assistants was totally different. Every assignment was the same politically. There was no promotion nor demotion for an assistant. The concern of this group focused on the kind of pastor he lived with and the kind of rectory he lived in. The church was non-spiritual and introspective.

Along came Vatican II which took the lid off Pandora's Box. This was the opening of the window to updating the church. Vatican II brought the role of lay people into proper prospective and emancipated the clergy from the slavery of confining protocol to the freedom of the sons of God who could now work for their people as the children of God. This can be described as the plurality of ministries. Parochially, the parish council emerged with all its commissions and departments and the involvement of the lay people in the running of the parish. The big word was delegation. This was now the age of the delegated parish. But was it? The hierarchy was accused of using Vatican II terminology with a pre-Vatican II mind set. They talked Vatican II, but they still thought in the context of a bygone age. Bishops spoke of the sufferings to the people caused by the implementation of decisions of the Council. They were mistaken. The decisions of the Council had been made and the people, the religious, and the clergy knew about these decisions. What caused the suffering in the church was the lack of implementation of these decisions. The level of frustration could be compared with the man who bought his wife a new car and did not let her drive it, and at the same time boasted about how good he was to buy her the car.

Similar frustration occurred in parishes. The councils were elected, commissions were appointed, and the word delegation became commonplace. But in some cases there was no greater delegation in the new structure than had been in the old. The pastor with new Vatican II terminology but the old pre-Vatican mind-set kept the same control over the parish that he had before. The difference was in the increased number of meetings he attended. Before, there were few meetings because there were no commissions. With the formation of the many commissions came many meetings. So the pastor attended every meeting to make sure that things would be done his way. He simply spread his thumb over a larger area. But it was still his thumb. The decisions he used to make at his desk now were made at commission meetings. This belies delegation. There is no delegation here. Some people say, "Man, this is great. We are really involved and active." Others say, "Let us not kid ourselves. Our only purpose is to agree with the pastor and to tell him what a great job he is doing."

Then there is the delegated parish. This is the parish where every department head actually runs that department and is responsible for its decisions. The principal of the school runs the school. The director of Religious Education directs religious education. The liturgist does the liturgy. The priests are responsible for the spiritual needs of the people. They do this wherever and whenever they are needed. Responsibility for each department lies with the department head, and department heads come together weekly for staff meetings to keep each other informed. It sounds great.

There are sufferings here, too. The first could be summed up in the statement, "The one who delegates is always suspect by the ones to whom nothing is delegated." This means jealousies within the parish and rivalries among the departments. At times, the pastor has to serve as mediator. Sometimes one department can take the bit in its mouth and run wild. The result is that the parish is thrown off balance. Further, there is the complaint of those to whom nothing is delegated. "Father, there are people in the parish making decisions that you ought to be making yourself." What this means is, "Let's go back to the good old days when Father made all the decisions and when we did as Father told us." This is the anti-clericalism that wants to imprison the priest once again in a cocoon of exalted non-personhood. There are moments of agony when certain people in the parish throw up their hands in despair and say, "What's the use? Father has turned the parish over to So and So and that is it."

Vatican II offered great promise to the laity and clergy. It liberated the clergy so that they could do priestly work. It brought the laity into a more direct service to the parish. But it brought its own sorrow. Many of the clergy left the priesthood because, when freed from the restrictions of the past, they could not handle the freedom or the responsibility without the old supports. Lay people discovered that participation in the running of the parish meant that Father shared authority with others, and that those "others" were not always the ones they liked most. The decisions made might not be what they wanted. They learned that delegation of authority does not always produce the expected results. Both clergy and laity have said, "We never thought it would be like this." Do we have a delegated parish? Yes, but it is often a difficult model. The church is a human organization. The parish is a human organization. Both are made up of some weak, vacillating human persons who try to do things right coming from their mutually–shared brokenness. The delegated parish is difficult to accomplish.

4

I Pray So Little

"Those who pray only while on their knees pray hardly at all." "Persons who pray for themselves only and for their own intentions pray not at all." These are two difficult statements for reflection.

Formal prayer is necessary and good. We must be faithful to our daily devotions – regular morning and evening prayers, meal prayers, and daily mass (if we have a schedule that enables us to attend mass, visits to the Most Blessed Sacrament, and the prayer of the liturgy of the hours). All these forms of prayer are good because we see in them the call of God.

Prayer is not our doing, but the action of God in us. When we pray, God initiates this response in us. We respond to the influence of God's grace in us. God summons us to our prayer.

Our prayer usually begins with a recitation of some formula or mantra that centers us in a state and attitude of prayer. Then our prayer becomes deeper and leads us into a state of quiet, listening to God as He speaks to us. Once I heard a lovely, holy woman say that she wanted to ask the priest something after mass, but she added, "He was getting his instructions from God." That is a beautiful description of prayer. We dispose ourselves to God and to listening to God's voice in our hearts.

Does such a disposition indicate that both clergy and lay persons are called upon to be mystics? The definition of mysticism is the "loving awareness of the presence of God." This loving awareness is at the heart of prayer. Everyone is called to contemplation, the highest form of prayer. We are all called to be contemplatives. The contemplatives are those persons who know what is going on without because they are listening closely to what is going on within. This attitude is opposed to the tunnel vision of hard-driving organizers who do not see anything nor anyone except their own immediate concerns. Contemplatives view the world and its concerns in a general way, usually not given to many details but with much understanding.

Thus, we are all called to be contemplatives, and we are all called to be mystics. This is another challenge because some of us by temperament have a difficult time being still, quiet, and deep-thinking. Some of us live on the ever-changing surface of the rapids where it is noisy and turbulent. That is one style of life. If we do not respond to our call to be comtemplatives and mystics then we limit our prayer life to formal prayers, and we will pray not at all.

I realize I pray so little, not because I don't go to mass or make my visit. I pray so little because there is so little of the loving awareness of God in my life. I am so distracted by the cares and concerns of work and play. I am so full of materialism that I am living on the surface of the crashing rapids. Once in awhile, I do rise above my own selfish needs and ambitions and give God a chance to speak to me. God always speaks, but sometimes his voice is drowned out by the roar of the noise of the world and my own internal noise.

When I come to formal prayer and try to settle down to clear the cobwebs out of my head, I am beset with the battering ram of the day's activities. I know that I am not the one to measure my own prayer nor the one to judge the quality of it. The judgment is God's. The intention and desire to pray are there. I know that the desire to pray pleases God. If I think I have had a poor prayer session, that does not matter. That judgment is not mine to make.

I feel that I pray so little because of the nature of the thoughts and plans that race through my mind all day. I am so self-centered, concerned with self-pity, my own schedule, my own everything. It seems to me I have a hard time praying in the loving awareness of the presence of God. But then, it is God who is the merciful one, the forgiving one, and the loving one. God is God and, therefore, it is he who continues to call me to a loving awareness of his presence in my life. His grace enables me to desire to respond. That desire is prayer.

5

I Exclude You
From My Life

O ur seminary professors had a most unholy custom of speaking only to the oldest student present. If a third-year man were engaged in conversation (small talk) with a professor, the professor had no problem in this situation. He directed his statements and questions to the third-year man. If a second-year man happened on the scene, no problem and no change. The professor spoke only to the third-year man.

But when a fourth-year man entered the picture, the professor spoke to him only. The oldest student became the object of the professor's attention. The sad part of this is that the third-year man who had been initially involved in the conversation was now left out and ignored. This behavior must have been based on policy, written or unwritten, because it was consistent in our seminary.

On one occasion, the priest speaker stated to the seminary student body, "I am addressing primarily the older men"; then he pointed to the lower classmen, "but you children may listen, too." In this case the "children" were mostly discharged military veterans with combat experience who might have been from five to ten years older than the "older" men. This insensitivity was sheer cruelty and mockery. But worst was that it was thoroughly enjoyed by the "older" men. It was taught to them and they learned well.

I recall a time when a newly-ordained priest from our seminary, a layman and I (I had just graduated from the minor seminary) were at lunch together. The conversation was primarily between the priest and myself. However, every question that I directed to the priest, he answered not to me, but to the older man who was with us. It was amusing because this third party was not the least bit interested in the subject and could have cared less. But the priest turned and spoke to him instead of to me. He answered all my questions, but not to me. A comedy scene could have been made of this if we had had video tape. It does serve to show how the practice of our seminary professors took hold of those they trained. The training was an indoctrination in subtle non-acceptance.

The reason I bring this up now is that this practice of speaking only to the oldest is really the practice of speaking only to the one I choose to speak to, to the one I have known, and to the one I allow into my life. This is the practice of "I choose to include this person in my life and to exclude that person from my life."

But this practice is not confined to the church. It extends into all spheres of life and to all people. It is evident when there is someone new around. It can be in the butcher shop where the new butcher approaches a customer and is told, "No thank you, I am waiting for. . . ." It occurs when the new service station attendant takes care of the car of the honored, long-standing, well-known customer. This customer and the other attendants converse, kid around, and completely ignore the new man who is aching for recognition and acceptance. The customer says goodbye and thanks to all the old-timers but does not acknowledge the new man and drives off. This is the same age-old practice of speaking only to the oldest, only to the ones we know, only to the ones we have allowed into our lives. On the other hand, it says to the one who is ignored, "I do not know you, and I refuse to accept you into my life."

Gregory Peck appears in a western movie as a seaman from the East. He is a stranger visiting a Texas ranch. (There is no greater stranger than a visitor to a ranch in Texas). One morning he is looking on as the ranch hands are hustling about getting ready for the day's work. He greets one man with "Good morning." The answer comes back, "Howdy." Another ranch hand passes by and Peck says to him, "Good morning." The man answers, "Howdy." Two cowboys walk past him and Peck greets them with "Howdy." They both respond, "Good morning, Good morning." This is funny but it is also sad. It is the same as saying, "We don't accept you into our lives or society."

"Remember that you yourselves were once aliens." Alien means stranger. This is our watchword in a sense. If we have to, let us recall those incidents when we were ignored, especially when we were ignored at the times when we most needed to be acknowledged. We can remember those times and then apply them to others. But this is backing into the real question. We ought not to need a reason for giving proper respect and attention to others. If it is proper respect, it is due them and from us. To ignore or slight someone because that person is young, new, weak, poor, or older is a crime. And for us to sit back and enjoy seeing another person ignored for any reason is equally serious. We cannot excuse ourselves. On the other hand, when we recognize a person and give him a respectful smile, nod, thank you, and most importantly, when we accept that person's offer to be of service to us, we accomplish more good than we can imagine.

It is then that we act like Christ. What would Jesus do? We know the answer and when we do it, Jesus acts in us all over again.

6

Pure As Angels
Proud As Devils

"*P*ure as angels – proud as devils" warns of building a spiritual structure on one virtue or building it on a narrow base. We are not to try to build a modern-day tower of Babel relying on our strength, efforts, and judgments. Let us go even more deeply into what this lesson can mean.

A person who may be greatly respected for holiness and spirituality but who at the same time is fearful of criticism, demonstrates a big gap in these virtues. One could wonder what holiness and spirituality are all about. If we isolate and insulate a person from reality because of the holiness of this person and because we are afraid of what this person will think or say, then we have created a false saint – a monster of our own deception.

If a person is known for an exemplary prayer life, for purity, knowledge of the Sacred Scriptures, and for the gift of praying in tongues, this is all good. But if at the same time that person is feared because of a sharp tongue, use of sarcasm or denunciations, then we must take a look at what spirit fills this person.

This is precisely what is meant by the expression, "Pure as angels, proud as devils." What good is it to be pious, devout, and holy if suffering and fear are left in the wake? What good develops if people suffer because of us and our misguided spirituality and purity?

I recall when I was a construction laborer a fellow worker told me that his mother-in-law repeatedly tried to break up his marriage. Then he added, "And she is a very good Catholic. That is why I am so down on the church." Many of us can see the stupidity of his statement. No good Catholic goes around trying to break up marriages. But this woman's attendance at Mass, her burning of candles, and her devotion to prayers, made her a good Catholic in his estimation. Hence come comments as "Why go to Mass? Only hypocrites go to Mass." These expressions come from a bad experience with people who have shown no gentleness and no compassion to go along with their piety.

We have observed with amusement the embarrassment of parents at a baptism when the baby has a bowel movement during the ceremony. Why the embarrassment? They are not embarrassed at home in front of the grandparents, but they are in front of the priest. They should be happy that the baby is not constipated, and unless the priest is constipated, he should not be affected in any way. This is natural and it is all right. The incident is funny and we should all laugh.

But this is not spiritual isolation. Spiritual isolation is allowing a person to set self on a pedestal of pristine purity and frighten everyone so that they not be allowed to get close to reality lest a speck of dirt get on the feet. This is spiritual phoniness. We all walk the same dusty streets and the reality of life is the same for all of us.

The day anyone gets so holy and cannot be shown the sufferings of others, whether that suffering be physical, moral or spiritual, the quality of the spirituality should be questioned.

When we are feared by others because of our holiness and our sanctity, let us toss that holiness out the window. Jesus was the holiest of all but the worst of sinners felt accepted and comfortable in his presence. Our efforts toward imitation of Christ is not the building of a superstructure of piety and devotion based on our own image of sainthood. It is in the imitation of his patience and acceptance of others.

The purity we speak of is good and we like it and want it. But if our holiness stops there, then it shows us that it is not enough. Another way of putting it is that purity without humility and kindness is worthless. In the great Broadway musical *Camelot,* Lancelot tells Guinevere that his strength and greatness are the result of his purity. She asks him if he has ever heard of humility. When he asks "What?" She responds in French. "Humilite." All his boasting about his purity left the rest of the people despising him.

In life we are faced with the same question day after day. We cannot push one aspect of our spiritual life and neglect the others. This is especially true of humility and charity. Without humility and charity we cancel out the other virtues. Jesus said, "No one can serve two masters." What he meant is that if we emphasize purity and prayerful devotion and forget humility, acceptance, and charity, then we are trying to serve ourselves first and God a poor second. It will not work. Thus, the purity of the angels will not even register against our pride of devils.

7

Depression vs. Sorrow

Jesus is known as the "Man of Sorrow" and Blessed Mother as the "Sorrowful Mother." But Jesus is not known as the "Man of Depression" nor is the Blessed Mother known as the "Depressed Mother." Neither person suffered from depression. Among the less informed, the word *depression* has a stigma attached to it – that of mental or emotional illness. Often, depression is the result of a physical illness. We speak of "post partum blues," of "post surgical blues," and other "blues" that follow a medical or traumatic experience. Often depression is glandular – the result of imbalance of the glands. Even certain back problems produce an effect that we call depression. This is why depression is often treated with medication.

Consequently we shudder when we contemplate that Jesus or that Blessed Mother were depressed. We do not like to think of them in these terms. We insist on seeing Jesus and Blessed Mother without equal as mentally and emotionally balanced. Neither suffered from a condition that came from within, yet both suffered from the circumstances about them. This is the difference. They did not go around with long faces. They were not gloomy people.

Yet, Jesus is the Man of Sorrows and Blessed Mother is the Sorrowful Mother. Sorrow is grief over suffering—both our own and that of others. Suffering results from being aware of what is going on about us. For this reason, only those who are aware of the sufferings of the world can be called people of sorrow. The insensitive person cannot be a person of sorrow because such a person does not feel grief over what others suffer.

Sorrow comes from *seeing* the sufferings of others, whether these people be close or half-way around the globe. Sorrow comes from *feeling* for others in their sufferings, and accepting our own sorrows. The person of sorrow will accept suffering as a necessary part of life without trying to escape it. Sorrow is being able to be crushed because we ourselves grieve and because others are immersed in grief or pain. This is the sorrow of Jesus who said, "My soul is sorrowful even unto death." At the point of his death, Jesus knew his own sufferings and the sufferings of all of us, and he also knew an especial appeal, "O My God, Why?" Jesus, who felt so deeply, could experience a sorrow that was so heavy it was able to kill him.

It has been said that greatness in persons is measured by the capability to bear sorrow. An immature adult will never be great because he cannot bear his sorrow and because he will never recognize the sorrow of others or suffer with them. He will remain a child—a "second-stringer" in the game of life without ever realizing it. Following Christ as the Man of Sorrows and entering into his sorrows will enable us to feel for others and to give of self for others.

Jesus says, "Be compassionate as your Heavenly Father is compassionate." The truly compassionate person is the person of sorrow. Compassion means to suffer with. But only the person of sorrow can suffer with another. If we are not truly compassionate the best we can do is look on from a distance, and give some advice from a practical standpoint. One counsel no one needs is that from a non-compassionate advice giver. Giving advice is a way of getting rid of something we don't want to deal with because we have no intention of entering into the suffering.

The marks of the person of sorrow are kindness, understanding, and acceptance. The person of sorrow does not merely tolerate others. This person accepts and tries to understand. As we grow older, and suffer and accept that suffering in our lives, we become more benign and kinder to others. There is a tendency in our youthful apostolic exuberance to confuse sin with suffering. This is one of life's necessary tragedies. But as we go through the "school of hard knocks" and accept the sufferings of our own life and the sorrows that come as part of those sufferings, the less we equate suffering with sin. Gentleness is a quality of the person of sorrow.

On the other hand, the depressed person filled with bitterness and despair can often be a source of real suffering. This person demands constantly. When we counsel depressed persons, we are concerned with the depressed person's need for revenge, retaliation and personal non-acceptance and self hatred. Sorrow has none of that. Depression reflects no happiness and is self-centered. Sorrow admits of happiness and allows others to be free and happy.

To be like Christ we must be persons of sorrow. There is much suffering about us. There are all kinds of sorrow which we must know, enter, and share. We must take up our cross daily and follow him. But there will be no way of doing this unless we enter the depths of the sorrow of the Man of Sorrows. The tendency to anesthetize ourselves with noise and "hoopla" in order to drown out the reality of the Crucified Christ is suspect. Liturgies and prayer ceremonies that appear to be artificial "New Year's Eve" tactics are often frequented by people who are fighting depression and who try to invent another narcotic – the religion of unreality. One of the surest signals of depression is seen in the person with the phony painted-on-smile who seemingly rejoices in everything, but really rejoices in nothing.

The "I will not suffer" syndrome is best translated, "I

am suffering but will not admit it, and please, somebody, help." Our first step to health is to admit that we are suffering. Our sorrow will be turned to joy if we accept the reality of life and unite our will to that of the sorrowing Jesus.

Simeon said to Blessed Mother, "Your own heart a sword will pierce so that through it the hearts of many may be revealed." Simeon predicted that she would be the Sorrowful Mother, but he gave the hope that through her sorrow, many would experience hope and consolation.

Jesus asked the disciples on the way to Emmaus, "Did you not realize that the Messiah would have to go through all these sufferings?" The fulfillment of the Divine Plan of Redemption necessitated the passion and death of Jesus. In both instances suffering was there. In both, glorification was there. In both there was sorrow, but in neither was there depression.

8

The Learned
and the Clever

"I thank you, Father in heaven, that you have hidden these things from the learned and the clever and have revealed them to the merest children." In this thanksgiving prayer of Jesus, we have a beautiful tribute to the childlike simplicity of those who live by faith. These persons accept the wisdom of God in their lives and live a faith-life that brings peace, love, hope to others.

Who are the merest children? Who are the learned and the clever? It is important to know because the learned and the clever have not received the revelation of the Father but the merest children have. We must find out who they are.

The child is the one who is in awe of all there is to be learned. The child looks with wonder at the world, listens with rapt interest to what parents have to say, and is eager to hear and learn. There is profound beauty in a child who asks and who trusts. Listening with intensity, what is heard is devoured. This is beautiful. The child is beautiful — teachable — coachable.

So long as we are childlike we will be teachable and we will be avid in our quest for knowledge because we know that there is so much more to learn and to know. The great minds of history were those who were amazed at how much more they had to learn. The true scholar knows that he has merely scratched the surface of knowledge. The scholar is indebted to the minds that have gone before. True scholarship is humility because true scholarship and true talent are humbling. The great television personality, Ed Sullivan, observed that you could always tell the "fly-by-night" from the master. He spoke of how Yehudi Menuhin practiced his scales before going on stage, whereas the instant success story with one hit song was unconcerned about practice.

The story is told of a college freshman who was expounding to a tired old man on a train about the scope of modern scientific knowledge that was now available to the world. He told the old man that new technological advances would eventually outmode the old man's thinking and belief. He was silenced when he found out that he was speaking to Louis F. Pasteur. The difference between scholarship and crass ignorance is best expressed by two expressions: "The empty barrel makes the most noise " and "Fools rush in where angels fear to tread."

In our modern society and religion, fundamentalist voices are on the rise. The unlettered and the unscholarly loudly and boldly challenge the masters of philosophy, history, theology, and Sacred Scripture. When a young fundamentalist told me, "I will stand up to anyone," I cringed at the thought. In his very limited learning he had arrived at the point where he thought he knew more than anyone else. This is total disregard for the centuries of thought, scientific research, and scholarship involved in examining the Scriptures. Nothing mattered to him because he thought he knew it all. He accepted no teaching. Scholarship is no match for ignorance of his type. He is unteachable.

Again, let us remember the prayer of Jesus. We ask who are the merest children and who are the learned and clever? A diligent scholar never claims to know all the answers. This person realizes that there is more to learn — that some knowledge will be elusive. The non-scholar is the one who "pooh poohs" knowledge, study, research, and claims that all knowledge stops with him. In reality, the non-scholar claims without saying it to be infallible.

On the other hand, when the unlettered lay claim to the inspiration of the Spirit even though they have not studied, the clergy is faced with a delicate problem. They have the right intention, but good intentions do not make for good teaching, nursing, bus driving, quarterbacking, or anything else. Good intentions do not count with a professor when one fails to do the assigned work or turns in a test paper that is all wrong. Should there be any difference in matters of religion? Knowledge is knowledge and talent is talent no matter where it is found.

The merest children are those who know that there is much more to learn and who stand in fear and trepidation at the thought of imparting knowledge to others because they know little. The "learned and the clever" of the Gospel are those who think they have nothing else to learn.

9

The Darkness of the Night

*I*n the beautiful book, *The Way of Divine Love,* Josefa Menendez constantly speaks of how the Sacred Heart of Jesus pleads with her, "Allow me the freedom to work in you." This is the definition and description of holiness. It is God who effects the work of our sanctification.

For years we move along in our work—praying and loving others, doing as much as we can for them, and fulfilling all of the precepts. We go to Mass, make our visits, pray our rosary, go to our prayer meetings and our Scripture classes. It is all good and it is all necessary because through sincere prayer and activity we prepare the soil for the Divine planter who will sow the seed and then give the increase. In all these years of prayer and activity we realize that we have only scratched the surface.

The preparation of the soil depends not on the number of Masses we have heard nor the number of novenas we have accumulated, but rather, it is the disposition to receive now what God has planned for us. It is the capability to allow God freedom to work in us, do his will in us, and thus accomplish in us what he wants. Consequently, it is God who gives us a college education. He does this by taking us to himself and leading us through the night.

We can describe the Dark Night of the Soul as the silence of God. It is the removal of the creature we had so depended upon either as consolation in prayer, or joy in doing good for others, or the removal of the supports we had so depended upon as the sign of our spirituality. Often it can be all of these and more. In the night we are brought face-to-face with God because the soul is directly involved and all the creature appendages have lost their effect and force. It is like the loss of an old friend. The loneliness of the night is intense.

Each person has needs, frailties, and strong points. The dark night for each person will be different. I like to think that the night is the strong point of the individual turned into weakness. It is the place of sorrow where each person is most confident and joyful because often we lean on our strong points and place great trust in creature so as to experience God directly without intermediary of creature. That very strong point must be removed, or at least made to be seen in its true light.

Is the night necessary? I think so. Without it we never would get past square one. The obstacle to our union with God is creature – any creature – ourself, other people, our own piety, work, success, ambitions – not being God, it is creature. And so long as it is creature, it can be a stumbling block. So the night is necessary.

We can make or break it in our dark night by our attitude. We can long for the onions of Egypt and want to go back to the days when our prayer was gratifying and our life manageable. We can rebel and lash out against others and against God. We can give up the ship. We can forget that we change because our experiences and sufferings have changed us. We can resist all of God's action in us, or we can, in the spirit of humility and trust, know that God is in command. We can submit to his loving providence knowing that through change, good is being accomplished. We are learning that we do not call the shots, that we are not in control.

It is in losing control – for ourselves and for others that we are helpless in a way that we have never been helpless before. At this time, we learn our greatest compassion through humility. When we know that we are being swept along by a force much greater than ourselves, and when we experience that force breaking into our lives, through the mediation of some other creature, we sink to our knees and reach out to God in the total darkness of our night. Then we see that we have tried to make it on our own, but that we have actually denied God. Many will come to this stage of life and prayer more than once. We will see our own will, intentions, and activities as actual denials of God. We will not arrive at this place through witnessing signs and wonders, but through the awareness that the "darkness of the night" is in reality the brightness of God. Then we will know that it is God at home in the core of our being.

10

Humility
Facing the Music

*I*f we want to practice the virtue of humility, we must face
the music, good and bad. That means facing the reality
of our life. We often pray for the grace of humility. We try
to cultivate it by meditating on the life of Jesus and the lives
of such saints as Therese, the Little Flower. But this is more
of a cultivation of ourselves in an ideal. It is a form of self-
achievement. We take some knocks that reveal that we did
not have much humility in the first place. The prayer, "Jesus,
meek and humble of heart, make my heart like unto thine,"
will be answered, but usually in an unexpected way. Often,
it is the prayer we utter when we are desperately in need
of humility after a humiliation. But it can also be spoken
when we are on top of the world and we don't want to get
proud and knocked off our perch. We want both.

   Humility is reality. Reality means facing the music and
calling the shots as they are. This is owning up to our
mistakes, failures, inabilities, and the way that these short-
comings are presented to us by others. Humility is not a ver-
tical virtue. It is horizontal. It does not deal directly with
God. "God is everything, I am nothing." That is not humility. But the ways we mess up in dealing with one another,

make others suffer, let others down when they depend on us, expect more for ourselves because we thought we were so good – these are cases for humility.

We need a good memory to keep a tight rein on our pride and to keep humility close by. We have to remember the many times we have failed others and ourselves by our stubbornness, or exaggerated sense of self-importance. Consider the times we crushed a grieving family because we insisted on protocol and did not consider their sorrow. Consider the times we failed to pick up on the needs of another because we were so busy concentrating on ourselves. Consider the times that we pushed others around and made them feel unwanted and unimportant. Consider the times that we actually despised those around us and spent our time bragging about ourselves and letting others know how much better we thought we were than they. These are the times that we inflicted deep wounds on others because we were filled with jealousy and hatred or because we were so egocentric that we did not care about them at all.

These are our worst failures. But it is necessary for us to remember also the ordinary mistakes that have caused others and ourselves embarrassment. We have all made mistakes and for some of them our faces are still red. They may have been innocent mistakes, and "if only we had known" etc. etc. But they happened. They were not selfish or malicious; they were just mistakes in judgment and for the most part they did not bring about anymore than a moment of embarrassment. For instance, thinking that a person is calling you and he is not. He is calling the person next to you, but you go rushing up to see what he wants. Or the times when you think, because of your own inexperience, that you are doing a person a favor but you are actually imposing a burden.

Mistaking the friendship of another for a deep-seated love and finding out that you are mistaken is embarrassing. Recall embarrassing cases of mistaken identity. We could go on and on. Each of us has a history of mistakes. It is good for us to keep them in mind because they are reminders. They have happened and they will happen again. Why does our judgment let us down now and then? Why do we say and do the wrong thing at the craziest times? Because we are human, our mistakes will be with us. The only way to make no mistakes is to do nothing at all and that perhaps is the worst mistake of all.

The other sphere of humility is the pain of humiliation through criticism. If we can accept the criticism of others when our failures are pointed out to us, and if we can accept what others tell us without bitterness and anger, then we are practicing humility. It is said, "If someone gets angry with you and tells you off, then quickly write down what he says, because that is what you are." Can we accept our failures as others tell us of them? Can we accept them as failures and try to improve on them without setting up all sorts of defenses and excuses and shifting the blame to others? This is the test of our humility.

This does not mean that we have to be "sitting ducks" for everyone who wants to take "pot shots" at us, but it does mean that our failures are seen by others. When we have failed, can we acknowledge that failure and accept it?

"Jesus, meek and humble of heart" is not much of a prayer when we are riding the crest of achievement and success and are hanging on to every bit of it. Rather, it is the prayer of our descent to the depths. We have to have a good memory to recall that descent.

But humility is not all bad. There is a beautiful, happy way to practice humility. That is to balance the memories of the ways we have been humbled by the beautiful things about us that we have been told. Compliments are especially gratifying when they point out qualities that we were not aware of ourselves, or when they show us that we have "come across" to them in a way that we never thought we had. When a compliment is a surprise – neither sought nor expected – then we are humbled and pleased. We must remember, too, that these are the times when we came across to others as making Christ visible in their lives.

The sweetest, gentlest way to be humbled is to observe someone who treats others with the love and tenderness of Christ himself. When we see individuals who are unselfish, then we are filled with a humbling spirit, and we can say that today we have seen Jesus. This is one of the easiest ways to learn humility.

11

A Love Like God's Love

When I was stationed at Sacred Heart Parish in the wind-swept plains of Willcox, Arizona, I noticed a particular winter phenomenon that occurred every once in a while. It began with a snow — a regular snow with fluffy, soft flakes that would fall silently and cover the ground. Then the next day was clear and bright and a hard, brittle, freezing wind would come and last all day. The effect of this wind was to dry up the snow until it looked like powder or flour on the grass. All the fluff, richness, and beauty were taken from it. It was dehydrated. But it was still snow.

In years of dealing with people in the sorrow of marital problems and the break up of meaningful relationships, I have noticed a similar phenomenon that occurs. We can draw a corrolary from what happens in relationships among people and what happens to the snow after the biting wind.

There is the love of marriage, or the love of friendship, or the love of meaningful relationships. These are like the silent snow. The hope, promise, and joy in these relationships are like the fluff and beauty of the snow as it falls and covers the ground.

Then may come crisis and trauma that result in heartbreak and the loss of trust and take away the hope, promise, and joy of the relationship. This despair is comparable to the hard driving dry wind.

This is what some authors refer to as the "Level of misery" in relationships. It is also very close to what happens in the dark night of the senses and the dark night of the soul as the consolations are removed from prayer. Satisfactions and gustos in relationships are withdrawn.

This might be the conversation in this situation.
"Does our relationship bring you happiness?"
"No."
"Do you trust me?"
"I find it very hard to believe you."
"Do you have any hope for our future."
"Not really."
"Do you want to recapture what we once had?"
"I don't know."
"Do you love me?"
"Yes."

As with the snow when the beauty of the fluff is dried up, all that remains is what makes snow snow. Happiness is taken out of the relationship. So what remains? It is the love that first formed the relationship. If this love is sustained, there is basis for formation of a true and lasting future relationship.

This basic love approximates most the love of God. It is the love that loves for the good of the other and asks nothing in return. In the human condition, it is the love that is based on the total emptiness of desolation. When we can love from the emptiness of that desolation, the sorrow is even greater. This love actually crushes, but is precisely the kind of love that sustained the wreckage of our broken dreams and expectations; we can build our greatest hopes for the present and the future—not founded upon our own strength, but upon the mercy and providence of God.

Can we not say that the dreams and hopes we once had were really our egoism imposed upon others, upon our present and our future? This causes us to be shattered when we are hit with harsh reality. When we descend to the level of misery, we are left with nothing except basic love. It is upon this love that we now rebuild a new level of trust in each other. This new level of trust is one of giving and depending. God does not tell us his secrets nor what he sees.

In relationships we have experienced our joys have been turned to grief, our hopes have been replaced by near despair, and the sweetnesses have become bitter. These experiences are like the dehydrated snow, but are the essence of love. It is from this point that we begin to build anew. Perhaps we can say that without these crises, we would never have known what true love is because it is in basic love that our love approximates most closely the total giving and forgiving love of God himself.

12

The Eucharist
and Faith

*A*ll the sacred mysteries surrounding the life and death of
Jesus were accompanied by external phenomena. When
he was born, there was the multitude of angels. At the
epiphany, there was the star. When Jesus was baptized, there
were the dove and the voice from heaven. When he was
transfigured, there were the voice and the dazzling garments.
All through his public life there were the miracles. At his
capture, those who came to take him found themselves
unable to stand up. There was the healing of the servant
whose ear had been severed. At his death there was the
upheaval of the earth that groaned and seemed to want to
self-destruct at the death of its creator. These events happened to help those present to believe.

There is one profound exception. When Jesus, the In-
carnate Word, chose to reveal the fulfillment of the mystery
of the Incarnation, he left its acceptance totally dependent
on the gift of faith, the darkness of faith. He gave no sign
and offered no wonder. He left those who heard him totally helpless. They had nothing to sustain them except the gift
of faith. This was not enough.

The people followed Jesus and they listened to him.

They accepted his miracle and the multiplication of the fish and loaves. There was more to come. There was the test that would separate strong believers from the unbelievers.

Jesus spoke to them of the bread of life. This bread, unlike the manna that their fathers ate, would keep them alive forever. They clamored for this bread. Yet, there was not faith. Then he told them of his greatest gift, the eucharist. But a gift is not a gift until it is welcomed and received and it was too much for them. The announcement had been preceded by the miracle of the multiplication but the multiplication of loaves was not enough and the announcement was too much. They could not accept it. Why could they not accept it? Was it that they were not holy enough? Not at all. They were *too* holy. When we rise above the gift, we cannot accept it. There was no test of faith before his promise, and thereafter there was not enough faith to accept it.

This happens often although we are unaware of it. It occurs often when we are given all kinds of gifts on the occasion of a birthday or anniversary. Then someone gives a gift that looks small and meager and "ungifty." We might smile and shrug it off. It is too small for us to accept as a gift. It is just no gift at all. Why? Because we believe we are too good.

Our reactions to gifts are similar to what happened when the words of promise were given. The people were too good, too holy, and too intelligent to accept such teaching. At this announcement, Jesus lost the first of his followers. They turned and walked with him no longer. He did not call them back. In fact, he turned to his immediate disciples and asked them if they, too, wanted to leave him and walk away. They could have, and maybe they wanted to, but Peter, the impetuous one, spoke for all of them, "Lord, to whom shall we go? You have the words of eternal life." The first break in Christendom came at that time of the promise of the eucharist. The next great break would come fourteen centuries later over the same question—the eucharist.

Today, the same crisis is upon us. We can call religious groups the "rapturists," or the "fundamentalists," or the "literalists," or the Pentecostals, but it is the same question. It will always be the same question. The greatest act of faith that God will ever ask of us is faith in the real presence of Jesus in the eucharist, as spiritual nourishment and as our friend in the tabernacle. Charles de Foucauld says that there is no test of our faith more demanding or greater than the adoration of Jesus in the eucharist. This is where the split in Christendom is evident once again.

The scriptural literalist believes as the Jews of the time of Jesus who wrote: This is a hard saying. Who can accept it? Like Thomas he says, "Unless I can put my fingers into his hands and my hand into his side, I will not believe." But there is no answer to the challenge. It is the very lack of faith that makes modern anti-eucharistic thinkers arise in adamant protest that since the eucharist is not visible, tangible, and readable, they will not accept it. This lack of faith is the off-shoot of the rationalism and positivism that arose in the last century in Europe and is now reaching our America. This rationalism almost eliminates the necessity for faith. Our present-day fundamentalist literalism is the last vestige of hope for one who is losing his faith to make a claim to faith. We call it literalism or fundamentalism, but it is the struggle for faith based on the lack of faith. Their rationale is stated: "Unless I see it written in the Bible, then I don't believe it. Show me in print, and then I will accept it. Let me see the chapter and the verse."

Faith is a gift, and the greatest act of faith is the faith in the eucharist. If our faith wavers it will show itself first in the loss of faith in the Most Blessed Sacrament. Why is it that some keep the faith and others do not? We don't know. But it seems that there is great hope. Those who have feared the loss of faith have, in all good conscience, tried to reach out for something to cling to and have agonized in their doubt.

Why is it that God has in his mercy allowed us to retain our faith in the eucharist – in the incarnation? We don't know. We are not to question it. But we marvel at the mystery of faith and we give thanks.

Blessed be Jesus in the Most Holy Sacrament of the Altar.

13

To Change People

Cardinal Ratzinger, in his book, *Faith and the Future*, writes very authoritatively that a person who is out to change others and direct and teach from a distance is doomed to personal and apostolic failure. The Cardinal makes a profound statement of the question of hatred, jealousy, bitterness, and non-acceptance. He is correct, but he does not go far enough. When we set out to change others, we directly and openly declare war on them and on their mode of being. We define our hatred of them and, in many cases, our hatred will be based on a feeling of jealousy that "they are what we are not."

Changing others is the philosophy of all that is not Christ. It is projecting ourselves as the ultimate masters of others and of how they should be. But that is only the disguise of the internal problem. The actual problem is that of self-hatred and internal frustration. Yet, this kind of thought and attitude comes forth at some board meetings. It is a font of profound sorrow to hear supposedly apostolic people affirm their positions as persons who must change others to make them better, or at least, make them different.

This attitude is headed for total failure and sorrow because it is the attitude of "I don't like you and I don't accept you. I will change you from this to that and after I

45

change you from this to that, I won't like you then either, and I will change you back from that to this. The important thing is that I will change you, and keep changing you, and will never accept you. The reason is, I hate you for being who and what you are and the reason for that is that I hate myself."

The "Let's-change-others" people claim to have knowledge that makes them superior and to have authority to direct others to greater perfection. It is difficult to accept such persons who have contempt for the values of others.

Contempt of others by some is why Christianity has had little success in certain parts of Africa where Christianity is identified with colonialism that despises African values and ideals. Colonialism is fraught with hatred and disdain, and replete with selfishness. Often our disdain of others is a way of excusing ourselves for the way we can exploit them and get the most out of them.

Colonialism is not restricted to multinational companies. It is practiced in our own society and in the church. When the officials of the diocese or parish look upon a certain group of people as those who have to be taken care of, they are exhibiting the paternalism that is characteristic of colonialism. When they designate certain members of an ethnic group as the "better" ones of that group, they separate that group of people. This is a form of colonialism. Also, when they refer to one group as "better," they make the remainder of that group the lesser. Who makes the judgment? Who is in charge? When someone tolerates these decisions and continues to be in charge, then what is the basis for that attitude? We all know. There is a certain satisfaction in making these judgments. There is gusto in being able to label people. But it is a sick gusto.

But what does all this reveal? It demonstrates our deep-seated bitterness and self-dissatisfaction as well as our non-acceptance of others. What is important is that we look deeply within ourselves and question what our attitude is toward others. If we want to change them, then let us beware. We are in trouble. Our purpose is to give others space so they may grow and be the beautiful people God created.

14

The Unbeatable Foe

*I*n one of the episodes of "Trapper John," the TV character Riverside was supposed to give a dissertation on how medical science had prepared people to protect themselves against nuclear attack. As he is giving his presentation, he points to a burn victim who had had four doctors, twelve nurses, and twenty-four hour care including all the latest medical technology. Yet, the burn victim died. Riverside continued his talk, explaining how we can successfully survive a nuclear attack – but stresses that with nuclear warfare *no one* wins. When it comes to nuclear warfare *everyone* is a loser. How true that is. Why should nuclear warfare have to be?

The whole question hinges on givers and takers. Again we have the question as to whether *anyone* wins or whether *everyone* loses. Why are there givers, and why are there takers? Why is it that some people are determined to win over others so as to be sure that they get ahead of others at all costs and by any means? Why is it that there are some who can be giving, but nevertheless are stepped on and pushed around all their lives? This is a mystery that starts in the individual lives of many and is projected into the corporate lives of national and multinational compaines. The greed and control syndrome of the great corporations that run our world today is the projection of the individual heart.

Against the "taker" there is no victory. Everyone loses. But who is the taker? The taker is the one who knows no other life in the world but his own, knows no other rights but self-rights, knows no other plan but own, and sees no other goal but self-good. There is no way to come out a winner over such a person. The taker is not a feeling person and the feelings of others do not register this person's awareness. The taker takes from others for self. The taker is the antithesis of the giving of Christ. The taker is a manipulator precisely because of being a taker. There is no such person as a sensitive manipulator. Sensitive people do not manipulate. There is no such person as a healing manipulator. Healers do not manipulate.

When we speak of total loss resulting from nuclear warfare and of the unbeatable foe, we are speaking of the non-giving individual who is matched against the giving individual. This could be compared with the boxer who enters the ring armed with cotton puffs while the opponent wears brass knuckles. Your argument is that you do not want to hurt him, but the opponent cares not whether he hurts you or how. This is the case of the giver against the non-giver or the taker. The taker has no feelings and takes advantage of the feelings of the giver and uses them to personal advantage.

What is the pay-off? The giver whether by win, lose, or draw, comes out the loser. The feelings of the giver for the sufferings of others cause grief. The taker then punishes the giver in having achieved some sort of a victory, if that be the case. But if the taker emerges victorious, then as victor he lords it over the giver and so punishes again. There is no victory over a taker. This person always wins. And the worst match in the world is to place a giver against a non-giver. The non-giver or the taker can take over behind an injury proofed shield of non-feeling, and make the giver feel like the worst possible rogue-lowlifer in creation.

Who is this non-giver and non-feeler? How will we

recognize such an individual? The non-giver can always be spotted by the following characteristics:

1) This person: Will always have others doing for self – may organize beautifully, but this always means that others break their backs doing what was planned by the non-giver.

2) Will always take credit for the good that is done – be it across the globe or wherever. Conversely, this person will never accept blame for any wrong doing or mistakes.

3) Behaves as though God, the world, and others always come secondary to personal wishes and intentions. The non-giver is first and others run a nebulous, faint second. This person's plans never change for the need or convenience of another.

4) Believes that the end justifies the means. This can include ridicule, lying, pressure, or anything else that achieves a particular goal at the time. It also can include "fence-jumping" according to convenience.

These are pretty hard forces to contend with. They are virtually impossible to conquer. The caring, giving person can be recognized by the cleats on his face, the footprints on his back pockets, and the empty bag he has been left holding so many times in life. One of the characteristics of the giving person is that that person is always doing for others.

So the greatest mismatch in the world is to pit a taker against a giver. The giver will be beaten to dust and demolished. The only match for a taker is another taker. At least they will use the same rules of manipulation and unfeeling.

We have often counselled people in marriage preparation. "If you are a morning person, do not marry a night person." But really we should say, "If you are a taker, then marry a taker and the two of you can be miserable with each other the rest of your lives." If you are a giver, then marry a giver and your lives will be as happy as can be imagined in this life."

This mystery of life brings to our attention the fact that God is in charge. Only the mercy and providence of God can unravel the mystery of the giver and the taker. We do not understand the reason why there are takers and givers. Many politicians government and church leaders are takers. Many of the great organizers and planners are takers. It is their tunnel vision that enables them to accomplish so much without being aware of the suffering that their energies cause others.

Takers are necessary. They are tempered by the givers who give to the world the stability, maturity, and spirituality that is lacking in the takers. We need both, but we are faced with the unanswerable question so often when we see them square off at each other. It is David against Goliath. How often does God intervene to allow David to win? The answer is not expressed easily. These are the times when we must trust and trust and trust. "My only answer is my prayers and my tears."

15

Jesus, Please Leave
So That I Can Speak to Jesus

*I*t is four o'clock in the afternoon and the time is here for the holy hour – a blessed hour of prayer, of silence, of listening and rest. It has been a rough day with many demands on time and energy. There have been appointments in the office – they usually involve sorrow and tension. As usual, the sick and elderly take their toll. I return to the rectory in time to see how many call-backs I have to make and to check the evening work schedule. I feel tired and I need some time. And now it is my time – time with Our Blessed Lord. Others have told me that it is not my time. It is really Jesus' time – his hour of adoration of his Eternal Father. I like that concept because it reminds me that I am not just receiving. I am also giving. Whatever, it is a beautiful time of day and I put on my prayer pants (jeans). I announce to the staff, "I am going to pray," and then I walk to the church where I will spend an hour with Jesus adoring his sacred humanity.

Then, guess what? There is someone waiting for me in the church. Everyone knows I am there at four o'clock, and they know where they can get me. So there they are. It is like another appointment. It *is* another appointment – except that the dialogues are whispered. The meeting can mean a problem, it can be for confession, or it can be an occasion to let me know what a mess I am making of the parish, or of my life. Does it matter? You bet it matters. It matters plenty. The time and energy it takes matter. I am knocked down, that matters, too. But the call is made, so it is up to me to give. My first reaction is to say, "Can't you see this is my time for prayer and silent recollection? Can't you see this is my time with Jesus?"

Oh, oh. That last line did it. I am refusing to see Jesus in this person who is taking my prayer time from me. In our seminary training, one of the things most impressed upon us was the concept of the "Sacrament of the Present Moment." This means that since this is the only moment that is from the beginning of creation to the end of time, we are to use this moment in the way God gives it to us. It is good and we should remind ourselves of that always. Another way that this is expressed is, "I fear Jesus passing." This means that the presence of Our Blessed Lord is here and now, in this situation, and in this person. It is terrifying to think that Jesus comes into our presence, and because of our previous plans, schedule, or self-importance, we fail to see him and we let him pass by. Our fists remain clenched and filled with nothing.

It is easy to see Jesus in the person of the sick whom we are called to minister to in the middle of the night. That is a cinch. It is easy to see Jesus in the next appointment in the office. It is a bit more difficult, but still not all that hard to see Jesus in the unscheduled caller who demands to see Father here and now. We have to remind ourselves that the beggar at the door is Jesus. After all, we have been schooled in that. But it is a definite challenge to see Jesus in the person who takes us away from our prayer and deprives us of our time of adoration.

Can this be Jesus who is taking us away from Jesus? Certainly it can be, and it is. This is Jesus who eternally adores the Heavenly Father through us. In our silent adoration he adores through us and through our adoration. Jesus actually adores the Father in us and through us. His adoration manifests when he tells us that today we will not get the time of rest and quiet that we want and need. He is here and we serve him in others, and he adores the Father in our service of others – in and through this interruption. So when there is someone waiting for us in the church who asks, "Father, have you got a minute?" we know that this is Jesus, The Eternal Adorer, who chooses to adore the Father in this way today. There is no way we can tell Jesus to go away so that we can speak to Jesus.

16

Rudolph and Bartimaeus

During the Christmas season we sing and teach the catchy little song, "Rudolph, the Red-Nosed Reindeer." It is a cute song with a delightful, easy melody. But if we look closely at this song we see the studied cruelty of an opportunistic society. The song "Rudolph" reveals the way we complacently accept cruelty and manipulation as part of our daily lives.

Let us take a good look at the lyric of this famous Christmas song. First of all, Rudolph is a freak. He has a nose that is an object of ridicule and mockery. He had a nose that "glows." Because he is a freak, he is made fun of. The other reindeer laughed at him and called him names. In addition, because of his deformity, they ostracised and exiled him from his society. "They would not let Rudolph join in any reindeer games." Because he is a freak, Rudolph suffered the humiliations of ridicule and mockery and the crushing sorrow of being cast out from his own kind. He was relegated to a life of loneliness.

Then one foggy night Santa comes to call. He singles out Rudolph precisely for his deformity – for his freakishness. He needs Rudolph because Rudolph has something that he can use for his safety and welfare. After this, the fortunes of Rudolph drastically change. "Then how the reindeer loved him." But did they love him? I doubt it. It looks as though they latched onto a good thing. When he was a poor, abandoned freak, no one had anything to do with him, but when he became famous – a celebrity – then everyone claimed to love him. But he was not really loved; he was only used. They jumped on the bandwagon of his fame and made the most of it.

As we teach our children this song, we could look around to see how many of them relate to it in the way the reindeer treated Rudolph. Many of our children see themselves as Rudolph. Today, some children dread going to and from school because of the treatment they receive from other children. They too are made fun of because they are not pretty, or they are not smart in class, or they are not gifted athletically; or above all, because they might be poor.

How many adults look back on their childhood seeing themselves, as Rudolph, taking childhood ridicule, and also see how when they became adults, that the kids they associated with as a child and who lorded it over them and made fun of them, now look up to them and admire them?

But in reality it is too late. Rudolph was not happy over the fuss the reindeer made over him after he hit the "big time." There was not love. There was no real appreciation. He was only a famous, useful freak. This same situation is present among many adults who might have a deep-seated mistrust of the praise of others because they have seen where it all comes from. Manipulation is not easily disguised.

So when we sing the song about Rudolph, and when we teach our children this song, we are showing them a cruel side of our society that we subconciously accept. And yet this is a song we sing at the joyous time of Christmas. Strange stuff.

And Bartimaeus is not much different. He is a blind, helpless beggar. All he can do is beg. When he cries out to Jesus for mercy, he is told by those around him to keep quiet.

Since they have the advantage over him they tell him, "Be still." He cries out all the more, "Jesus, Son of David, have pity on me." Jesus hears him and calls him over. Then the people rush to the aid of the blind man and reassure him as they help him up saying, "Don't worry, you have nothing to fear from him." Notice that before Jesus noticed him they were telling Bartimaeus to keep still; now they rallied around to be the ones who help and encourage him. They jump on the bandwagon and latch on to the fame of the celebrity. Notice the similarity between Bartimaeus and Rudolph.

We don't hear anything about Bartimaeus after this incident. He probably did not have any marketable skills and very likely after being Bartimaeus, the blind beggar, he was relegated to being Bartimaeus, the sighted beggar. With the attitude of the bystanders who used him and who changed their views toward him in a split second, it is reasonable to suspect that they abandoned him just as quickly after he was cured. If they could step on him before Jesus called him, then come to his aid after Jesus called him, they had more concern for themselves than for him. When he was no longer useful to them, they just left him.

Rudolph and Bartimaeus – the same story – a story that is retold over and over again in our society.

17

When I Needed
You Most

O ne of the greatest remorses comes when we rebuff, re-
ject, and ridicule those who love and need us. In the
marriage instructions we make that point most strongly. This
person we are to marry should be *numero uno*. This person
is the number one person in the whole world, in our life,
because this person places hope for happiness in our hands.
This person gives us the heart for safekeeping and reminds
us that we are to handle it with care because it breaks so
easily.

We are responsible in a way for the feelings of everyone. Just sit in a booth of a hamburger stand and observe
the people who come in. Do they come in alone or with
others? Are they silent or conversing with a friend? Let us
take a couple of seconds to reflect on the depths of their feelings and of the need they have for reassurance. Many times
our smile may shock and surprise them, especially if they
are struggling with hurt or bitterness or doubt. More often
than not, our look of friendliness and our smile will do much
to make total strangers just a little happier that day. We may
not even look at them, but if we look happy then we can
have a good effect. Many people are hurting in so many dif-

ferent ways—from loneliness, fear, poor health, or tensions of home and work. They come into our presence for healing. This is not the cure of a physical sickness, but the healing of spirit and heart that can lead to other kinds of healing.

An incident that sets us off in a bad way may be imperceptible. An incident that restores our spirits can be just as imperceptible. We might be in a very down-mood all day and not know why. We know that we did not start off the day depressed, but that is the way we are now. If we could retrace our steps with minute by minute precision, we would probably come to the recollection of a contact with another person—a friend, a stranger, loved one—and therein see why we changed our mood. Something was said, done, or just sensed. That did it. The "vibes" were not that good: "I felt your tension. I felt your displeasure. I felt your silence." These things can scream at us—not in our ears but where we live; down deep. The effect will be undeniable.

Have we not often announced that the clerk in the store or in the post office is so pleasant? This person has a good effect on us. In the same way, we are all responsible for the feelings and the happiness of everyone we meet. These people are the little ones and Jesus has told us that so long as we receive one of these little ones in his name, we receive Him.

The main point here is that we can do penance the rest of our lives, like Peter who "went out and wept bitterly," for the way we inflict suffering on those closest to us. A few hours before, Peter had made the bold statement that he would die for Jesus if he had to—that he would never deny his Lord. However, when the occasion arose, Peter denied that he had known Jesus. Then he heard the cock crow and he remembered his words. That did it. Why did Peter weep so bitterly? Jesus had already predicted the denial. He had a hint of the denial, but when he made his promise, he had every intention of keeping it. At the moment of the denial, Jesus did not come to Peter and say, "Peter, tell them that you are my friend; tell them that you will lay down your life for me." Jesus did not approach Peter or ask for anything.

Peter got off easy. He lived a life of remorse for having denied his Lord. However, his situation is not as difficult as the experience of many of us who have made a similar denial when the person we denied was the one who loved us most, trusted us most, and needed us most. A great sorrow in life is the remorse of the one who is told, "I needed you, I trusted you, I came to you filled with confidence, hope, and expectation. I was met with your rebuff, your denial, and your rejection.

Peter got off easy. Jesus had already told him what he was going to do. Peter just forgot. Our situation is different and much worse. We have to face those who needed us, and who came to us in that need confident that we would be there for them in consolation and support. Thereafter, we are obliged to live a life of profound penance, looking deep into the eyes of that person, knowing that we have inflicted wounds that will never completely heal. Maybe we can't treat these wounds. Maybe we can ignore them. Maybe we can try to make up for them, but we know that such wounds will never really heal.

Sacred trust or love is terrifying. The wounds of love are, too. However, the greatest healing is yet to come when the wounded becomes the healer.

18

And I Will Give You Rest

"Come to me all you who labor and are overburdened and I will give you rest. Learn from me for I am meek and humble of heart and you will find rest for your souls."

How often we speak and pray these words especially in times of distress and sorrow. We believe that the words and promises of Jesus will be fulfilled. We believe that he will come to our aid and be the rest and the consolation for our souls.

The quandry is that Jesus does not give us any other answers. He tells us that he will give us rest. He will be the comfort for us in our sufferings. He does not tell us how or when. He promises us rest, but he leaves us up in the air – waiting. He says, "Come to me " and that is it. We are to take him at his word. We are to await his consolation and his peace.

Most of our sufferings are the result of our having loved. The sorrow of grief is the sorrow of love. We cannot love without suffering. Suffering is the by-product of our own loving. It is not to be expected that the sorrow that comes as a result of our having loved should be taken away quickly. If we have loved, we will suffer and grieve. The two go together. The more we have loved, the greater will be our grief.

This is when we must live by faith. Jesus has promised us that if we come to him, he will be our help. But since he does not tell us how he will help us, we have to live by faith and allow him in his time to fulfill his promise.

We are reminded that it is the direct work of God in our souls that will turn our sorrow into joy. There is no human consolation that can be a substitute for his action in us. We must then live in patient conformity awaiting his consolation as the aged Simeon awaited the consolation of Israel.

For those of us who have been faced with crushing sorrow, and who have taken these words of Jesus at their face value, we know that Jesus is as patient in fulfilling his promise as he is firm in telling us to live by faith and confidence in that promise. If we choose otherwise, we let ourselves in for even greater suffering.

19

Self-Image

Two of the greatest characters of the Christian Bible are known for their strong self-image. They are John the Baptizer and Jesus. Both knew who they were and what they were all about. They made no pretenses as to their person or their mission.

John announced that he was the voice crying in the wilderness, that he was not the messiah, and that he had to decrease. He had a strong self-image, and he possessed nothing. With some of the disciples, he lived a life of poverty and austerity. He told the other disciples to follow the Lamb of God. John was a man of great courage. He asked nothing for himself, and he did not live under any pretenses.

Jesus knew who he was and he was able to claim for himself the role of prophet and to experience rejection in his own hometown.

Self-image is often misunderstood. We like to think of it as an idea we have conjured ourselves. No way. Self-image does not come from looking into a mirror, nor by reflecting on our own daydreams. Self-image comes from what others tell us about ourselves. If people tell us how good we are, that we are loved, we are doing a marvelous job, we are admired and sought after for this or for that, and if we believe them, we will have a good self-image. It is not to be confused with pride. On the contrary, self-image comes from what others have told us.

If others tell us we are a "lousy hunk of nothing," no good, not loved, and if they indicate to us that we are not appreciated nor wanted nor respected, and most especially, if we are ignored, and if we believe all this, we will have a poor self-image. This is not to be confused with humility. In fact, it is the person of poor self-image who is often the most filled with pride. If we are called winners by others, we will feel like winners, and if we are told we are losers, we will feel like losers.

The person with a good self-image is able to live life without having to prove worth and presence to self and to others. The person with the poor self-image has to boast, show off, and make vain comparisons in order not to be left out or to be unnoticed or to be lost like the proverbial "needle in the haystack."

The person of good self-image will always be able to give and to serve. The person of poor self-image will continually grasp and clutch and demand to be served.

So what do we do about the good self-image and the poor self-image? We must face reality. In order to establish a good self-image we must recognize who we are and who we are not. We cannot fabricate talents and abilities that we do not have. We have to know ourselves as the beautiful persons God made us. We cannot deny his creation by trying to be what we are not. This exhausting effort reflects a poor self-image.

We must foster good self-image in others. We must know them as the beautiful people God made them, and we are to let them know they are beautiful and good. This is not seduction. We are not to lie about it. If others do not have certain talents and abilities, and if they are not close to us, it is destructive to "butter them up" and build them up for a crash.

Bishop Patrick Flores once pointed out that in certain

parts of Texas it was school policy not to grade or flunk Hispanics. They would be promoted automatically all through school until they graduated from high school despite a third grade reading level. Now that is dishonesty and it is seduction. Such deceit is not redeemed by claiming encouragement.

Our attempts toward building a good self-image in others must be based on a sincere recognition of their talents. Just as people are not allowed to claim talents that they do not have, we are not allowed to let them think they have talents they do not have.

There are people who have a poor self-image because no one ever tells them anything good about themselves. If other people tell us good things about ourselves, let us hope that they are sincere. Let us rejoice for the good they have found in us. Let us, in turn, seek sincerely the good in others and tell them of that good. But above all, let us never deceive them nor seduce them.

20

Love Feedback

"By this will people know that you are my disciples, if you have love one for another." Our Blessed Lord does not mince any words in this admonition. He lays it on the line. The badge of our following of the crucified Christ is our love of one another. It is not our uniform, our title, our position in society or in the church. Much less is it our claim to be his followers. Our love is the sign.

Apostle John tells us that we cannot claim to know the love of God until we have known what it is to love another person. "No one has ever seen God. But if we love one another, God will live in us and his love will be complete in us."

We all claim to fulfill the words of the Gospel and the words of the letter of John. There is no problem in what we say about ourselves. If someone were to ask us, "Are you a follower of Christ? Can we recognize you as a Christian by the way you love others?" our answer would be, "Yes, of course. I am a loving, giving, sensitive person and I do love and this is the way I live my Christianity." No problem.

We are not the judge of our own Christianity and our own spirituality. We are not the doctor in our own case. If we really want to find out what kind of Christians we are, if we really want to know just how spiritual we are, then

66

let us bounce the question off the people who are closest to us. These are the people who are the most accurate barometers of our following of Christ.

We might insist that we are the model of Christian living and loving. In fact, there are some individuals who would go into a life-long pout and sulk so as to force us to tell them that they are Jesus of Nazareth. And heaven help us if we don't. Realistically, it might be an abrupt awakening if our friends and relatives risked letting us know just what kind of Christians we are. It is not for us to proclaim how holy we are, how prayerful we are, and how loving and giving we are. It will be told to us if we have the courage to ask and the humility to accept the response. Let us ask our spouse, brother, or sister. In sincerity, let us ask if we are followers of the loving healing Christ.

The words of Jesus tell us that it will be others who will know whether we are his disciples or not. It is not for us to make that determination. Others will know if we are, and they will tell us.

21

Busy

vs.

Busybody

*J*esus was so busy taking care of the people who came to
him, that he and his disciples did not even get a lunch
break. When his family saw this, they went up to him and
tried to pull him out of circulation to take care of him. They
were sure he was out of his mind.

That is amusing because Jesus was not acting like a
crazy man, but as a sane person. But he was busy, so busy
that he was not getting a rest-break, and he was working
himself half to death. He knew what he was doing, and he
was doing much good. The people were coming to him from
all sides and they needed him and what he was able to do for
them. He was not multiplying unnecessary work. He was
always busy because work makes for more work.

The problem was not with Jesus. The problem was
with his family. They imposed their limitations on Jesus.
Jesus had the energy, strength, and zeal to work hard and
to get much done. His family members did not have these
qualities. But since they could not do for themselves, they

tried to move in – in busybody fashion – to try to stop Jesus from doing.

Hence, even in the days of Jesus and even in the closeness of his family, we find the difficulties of the emerging head and the tendency to lop it off by not minding one's own business. Jesus was able to do and was doing; others tried to stop him from doing. There was a problem, but the problem was not with Jesus. They said that he was out of his mind, but it was not Jesus who was out of his mind, it was the family. They were not thinking right.

We see this again and again when we find very active efficient persons who can get lots done in their own way. It may not always be orthodox according to some standards, but they are able to accomplish much and these accomplishments are good for many people.

Watch out for the "do nothings" and the "have nothings." They move in with ostensibly good intentions and throw monkey wrenches into the machinery by uncalled for meddling that takes time and energy and waste both. By this you will know the uninvited meddlers and the "have nots" who use the expressions: "Why don't you?" and "You ought to." Now all progress stops. What remains are the spinning of wheels and the racing of the motor. Activity is reduced to expending energy in explaining modes of action to someone who does not care anyway. Most busybodies don't care what you do. All they want is that you wear yourself out justifying yourself to them. This is a killer.

Let's turn this around and check ourselves to see how many times we demand explanations from others about what they are doing or not doing. How often do we suggest something else to them merely for the sake of adding a burden to their lives? We become burdens in the lives of others when we deliberately show our non-acceptance of them by "nit-picking" over some issue that does not concern us at all. If they can do a task and do it well, then let us leave them alone and allow them to do it, and ask God to bless them.

The family of Jesus moved in like busybodies to take charge of him. They thought he was out of his mind. No more has been told to us about the situation. I think that Jesus let them know in no uncertain terms that it was not he who was out of his mind. Were they, his well-meaning family members, out of their minds?

22

Sensationalism

*T*he story of Naaman, the Syrian general, is a great one for us if we are given to sensationalism in our religious practices and devotions.

In the story, Naaman is afflicted with leprosy. The slave girl in his house tells him to go to the prophet, Elisha, to be cured. He goes to Elisha with a large retinue taking with him all sorts of gifts. He arrives at the prophet's house but the prophet does not make an appearance. The prophet had sent word for Naaman to go wash in the river Jordan seven times. What a let-down. So Naaman, the important general of the Syrian army, becomes indignant and is highly incensed. He riles about the simplicity of the answer. It is too easy and it is too simple. Since he is so important he feels that he deserves something better, more complicated, and splendorous. He complains that the prophet neither comes out to pray over him nor to touch the malady. He decides to leave in his leprous condition. That is how angry he is.

It is then that his friends and servants step in and tell him not to be a sap. What does he have to lose? He expected to be treated with more attention. He figured that he, in his illness, deserved greater attention. It is too simple to make any sense, and now he is not making any sense. They tell him to do what the prophet said to do. They tell him to forget his pride and his self-importance and accept the simplicity of the advice. He does this, and is cured.

Often this is our story. Not only do we do this with God but with others. We cannot accept the good and simple. Circumstances have to be flashy, grandiose, and spectacular lest they be beneath us.

God's grace is simple, quiet, gentle. Solutions to many of our problems are there and they too are gentle and simple. Our problem is that we think we are too good and too noble for the simplicity of it all. We also think that our problems need special attention.

I always shudder when people tell me that they prayed and God told them this or that. What they usually mean is, "I prayed to myself and I told myself something about you and about what you should do." It is interesting how the "God told me" people can always tell others what to do. They seem to have an "in" with God on how to run the lives of others.

Today our religion has taken on much of the noisy and flashy. The danger is that we have put so much creature into our religion that we have crowded God out of it. Naaman wanted so much creature satisfaction and grandeur in his cure, so much flash and splash that he almost neglected the grace and the power of God. That is our danger, too.

23

Sensitivity to Suffering

"*I* realize that if I had prayed more and better, if I had been more in touch with the Lord, I would not have the intense suffering that I have now. I would be hurting less."

This is one of the great fallacies that perseveres throughout the ages. The fallacy is that if we are holy, we will not suffer; if we are close to God we will suffer less. This makes the grace of God and his life within us an anesthetic—a spiritual Novocain. Actually the opposite is true. Holiness increases the capacity for suffering. Jesus was the holiest of all and because of his holiness and his perfection, he was capable of suffering more. To be like Jesus means that the closer we come to God, the more sensitive we are to pain, sorrow, grief, and rejection.

Our greatness is measured to a degree by our capability to bear sorrow. This is what distinguishes the king from the brigand. Nobility is being able to bear sorrow with dignity and honor. The greater the perfection of creation, the greater the capability for feeling and hurting. The cricket does not have the capability for suffering as does the human. Some of us remember being slapped across the hand with a ruler when we were in grade school. The hand is tough and does not have the delicacy of the eyes. If we had been hit with the ruler across the eyes, there would have been a much greater and longer-lasting suffering.

The closer we come to the centrality of life and love, the more qualities of perfection we assume. Jesus, who was closest to the Father, possessed qualities of perfection and the greatest capability for suffering. His prayer of fear and sorrow in the garden and his bloody sweat showed how much he could suffer. His holiness did not spare him grief at the death of Lazarus. His holiness did not enable him to shrug off the betraying kiss of Judas or the panicky denial of Peter. Rather, because of his holiness and closeness to God the Father, he was more sensitive to pain and sorrow.

Presently, there seems to be a movement afoot to recite Psalm 23 as a guarantee that faith and hope preclude suffering. I was once told, "If I have faith in God, I know He will take care of me." Sure, God will take care of us. But He did not make us indestructible and we are all going to die. Dying is not easy. Rest homes give witness to the prolonged sorrow of the helplessly aged. Hospital wards — cancer, orthopedics, surgery, emergency — all departments of our hospitals — tell us of the pain of death and dying. We are all dying and dying is hard. Many times there is suffering in the dying process. If we live long enough, our bodies wear out and we die.

No amount of holiness will prevent this reality from happening. There is the daily death and dying that we all go through in order to rise again. It is the frustration, disappointment, loneliness, and struggle that is part of our everyday condition. No amount of holiness will prevent this reality. It is the reminder that this world is not our eternal home. I have heard people say that they want to be like Adam and walk in the cool of the evening with God and never suffer. Good, so do I. But that is not the reality I must face everyday which is that God has not promised me a rose garden, but He has promised life eternal.

When I hear others say they would not have suffered

so much in a past tragedy had they been filled with the Holy Spirit, all I can answer is, "Perhaps not. But I think the suffering would have been greater. The difference is that you would not have rejected the suffering as you did."

Faith and grace do not take away suffering. Rather, they enable us to accept suffering and live with it and grow through it to become what God wants us to be.

24

Hate Level
Love Level

"I hate this, and I hate that with a 'purple passion.'" How often do we hear talk like that? It sounds harmless because it means that we dislike something or that we are "turned off" by it. But hatred is the wishing of evil. Everytime we use the word "hate," we raise the hatred level worldwide.

With our automobile emissions tests, we are conscious of air pollution. We breathe the pollution around us. It becomes part of us. Therefore, it is important that we take care to ensure that our air is clean.

The same holds true for hate pollution. Everytime we use the word "hate," we raise the hate pollution of the world. Everytime we get angry enough to use that word, we infect the air around us with our own internal discord and lack of peace. People around us must then live in an atmosphere of tension that we have created. They have to breathe our hate and anger. We have lowered their peace and love level.

The doctrine of the Mystical Body of Christ, is that everyone draws from the general health of the Mystical Body of Christ, the Church. Thus, when one member suffers through sin, the entire body suffers just as when one member of our physical body suffers through pain, the entire body

76

suffers. If we drop something on our foot, then the eyes go down to see, the hands rush to hold, and the entire body "scrunches" around the injured member to bring healing and consolation. The whole body suffers. When one member of the body suffers, the health of the entire body is affected, and the health level is lowered. So it is with the Mystical Body. We all depend on the health of that body through grace and love. When there is sin in that body, there is disease and we all suffer.

And what is sin? Sin is the failure to have loved. Sin is hatred, anger, and malice. Sin is blocking the peace, healing, and mercy of God in our world. God pours forth love and forgiveness into us and our world. It is there. All we have to do is accept it in our lives. The opposite of this peace and love is discord and hatred. When we love, we allow God's love in the world to flow into ourselves and others. When we fail to love, we stop that flow. The health of the Mystical Body depends on the flow of love and peace from God. The more we love, the more that love is free to flow. The health of the entire body is raised because the love-level is raised. Conversely, when we fail to love, when we hate, or when we allow anger to overcome us, the general health of the body is lowered. We are least Christlike when we are angry. When we let ourselves get out of control in anger, even our physical appearance changes, and we lose our beauty. The angry person is ugly and causes fright and alarm in others. Notice how tense the situation can be when one person is angry. Fear enters the hearts of those around. From this anger comes hatred. Anger seeks revenge, and hatred seeks to do harm. Both damage. Both are infectious. When President John F. Kennedy was shot, a TV commentator gave a marvelous editorial, "Let's cut out the hate talk." He cited the statement, "All the Kennedys should be taken out and shot." Hate breeds further hatred. A person who hates and talks about this hate, does not nurture peace and love. When we speak of hate and express our hate, we fill the air with hate and expose the minds of others to our hate.

There are many things we don't like. If we don't like something—all right. We can say that "Hard rock music gives me a headache." A person told me once, "I hate all sports." That is silly. Does he mean that he would wish the destruction of all sports and the obliteration of the memory of sports from the earth? No, he means that he is not athletically inclined and that he dislikes exercise and activity. But the damage is done. When we use the word "hate," we fill the air with a negative charge and that results in harm. In one way or another it lowers the peace level around us. This is true even in allowing ourselves to feel hatred. This electrifies the air around us with its destructiveness because hate is destructive.

On the other hand, love builds, restores, and heals. God is love; he who lives in love, lives in God. We bring peace to those around us by our acts of love. When we speak of what we like, this heals. Of course, we cannot speak of what we like when we know it just grates on someone else. That is cruelty. When we love we build the level of love and peace throughout the world for which we are responsible. We make peace by our acts of love, thoughts of peace, and our prayer. We raise the love level. We enrich the health of the entire Mystical Body of Christ by our love.

25

Losing Faith?

"*F*ather, I have a malignancy and I have put all my trust in God's mercy and I pray and pray and pray. Yet there does not seem to be any improvement and now I am afraid I am losing my faith." Is this person losing faith? No. There is a tendency to equate faith with assurance that what we ask will be granted in the way we ask. We know our needs and our intentions. But we don't necessarily know God's will. We know that God wills the best for us. But this "best" is hidden from our eyes. We do not see with the eyes of eternity. So we do our best, and that is all we can do. However, if we doubt that God wills our cure, healing, or anything else we pray for, that is not necessarily loss of faith. There is a genuine doubt as to whether or not God and we are on the same track. A person who prays more especially when things look their worst is not losing faith. It comes down to, "I really don't know whether I will get well or whether I will die from this."

Please pray for my children. Not one of them ever goes to Mass anymore. I am afraid they have lost their faith." Here again, we have a case of misused terms. This is often the case with young people in their "U" curve situation. They have not lost their faith. They still believe in God and trust in God and pray in their own way. They just don't like going to church. They are "turned off" by the Mass. They find it boring and unmoving. It does not speak to them. But in reality their faith is intact. The issue of church attendance is something that will have to be worked out in time – mostly their time – and in getting the church to make worship come alive for our younger people.

Older people who struggled through the years of the Baltimore Catechism in its cocoon-type existence felt "different from other people because they were Catholics." These people might now say that they have lost their faith because of the changes since Vatican II. They might use expressions like, "I have to unlearn everything I was taught". Of course, it could be that they never went beyond fifth grade catechism. Also, the liturgical changes can make it difficult for some of our seniors who had been happy to come to Mass, pray the rosary, or follow the missal in silence. With other changes: singing, and the responses, the handshaking, the preaching on social justice instead of on the salvation of souls; some older people find themselves upset over the way the church is going. And the ecumenical trends do not help them either. Some might even think they are losing their faith. They are not. They are merely finding it hard to accept the liturgical and ecumenical innovations. Even if they no longer want to go to church, they are still not losing their faith. In fact, it is because their faith and love are strong, that they grieve so much.

Another instance of fear of losing faith is expressed: "I can't pray anymore. I used to pray easily and freely and it was such a joy. But now I can't pray anything. I try one thing after another and nothing works. What is wrong? Am I losing my faith?" The answer again is "No." The person who is losing the gusto of prayer life and finds it impossible to pray as in the past, might very well be advancing from a more structured prayer to a more simplified prayer. This is not easy. There can be much suffering involved, but there is certainly not a loss of faith. Here again, the agony associated with prayer shows that there is no loss of faith.

This person's faith is alive and vibrant. It might be, too, that the individual is growing careless and merely allowing laziness to take over without having made real effort to be open to God's action in life. The person who is concerned over difficulties in praying, and who asks the question "Am I losing my faith?" is not losing faith.

"No, we don't go to Mass. We used to but we are not married in the church, our case is an impossible one, and we cannot approach the communion table. It is such a sorrow of loneliness and emptiness to sit in church and watch the other people go up for communion, that it is easier not to attend at all." Is this person losing faith? "No." There is a great faith demonstrated here. This individual's love and desire for the eucharist make it a profound sorrow to see others have communion. It is like sitting down to a meal and not being allowed to eat. It is easier to stay away. This is sorrow, but it is not loss of faith.

Another person who might question the loss of faith is that person who questions the problem of evil and suffering. This is the individual who asks, "How can God permit suffering, injustice and cruelty in the world? Is he cruel or is he indifferent? I just can't figure it out." This is a legitimate question and many ask it when they see the sufferings of our world, and especially when the innocent are in the hands of the uncaring. But if we all had the faith of the questioning individual, we might have lots going for us. This person sees suffering, suffers with the suffering, and asks "Why?" There is deep faith here. It is the kind of faith that lives and moves. It is the type of faith that Saint James tells us we must have. Thus, when we hear a person ask these questions, we know that we are in the presence of a person of faith.

Just who is losing faith? Very simply, it is the person who is agitated and anxious within and is constantly battling and arguing with self and others about matters of faith. This is the person who, like the Apostle Thomas, will not believe unless "he can place his fingers into the spot of the nails and his hand into his side." In other words, it is the person who will not believe but must have everything shown in "black and white" so not to believe. This is the individual who has to have total security so as not to have to take the step into the dark. This person, in a state of unrest, worries and frets constantly and asks questions like, "Where is it in the Bible? Show me the chapter and verse." The people of the time of Jesus kept asking for signs so that they could see and thereby believe. Actually, when we ask for signs, we are weak in our faith. Asking for signs is a sign in itself. It is a sign that we are losing faith. When we can no longer believe, we must see; and if we cannot see, we no longer believe.

Faith is intimacy with God. It is this definite familiarity with God that allows him to take over completely in our lives because we cannot do ourselves. A person of faith faces something much too great and rejoices. This intimacy produces a certain calm and certainty. If we begin to lose our faith, we lose that intimacy, calm, and certainty. We become agitated, ill at ease, nervous, and jumpy. Jesus tells us, "Let not your hearts be troubled. Put faith in God and faith in me." The troubled and restless spirit is present in the one who does not believe. The one who believes accepts on faith and is happy. There is a big difference.

26

Alone and Empty

Who is lonely? Everybody is lonely. Aloneness and emptiness are part of the human condition and are present throughout our lives. There is the loneliness of teenagers who do not know what is going on. They wonder why they are different from everyone else. There is the loneliness of mid-life that looks back at unfulfilled dreams and looks ahead to old age. There is the terrible suffering of the loneliness of old age. This is the emptiness of feeling useless and unwanted that is part of growing old. The feeling of aloneness and emptiness is a sorrow that all of us need to be aware of and enter into as a part of life.

Loneliness is experienced by everyone at various times in life. It comes to us in different expressions and intensity. There are times of rapid and slower growth in our lives. Each stage brings its own kind of loneliness and emptiness. We experience loneliness in the different stages of our lives. We experience it according to our particular situations and attitudes at the time.

Loneliness is like a wall that has a brick missing. It remains a wall but there is something lacking in the wall that should be there to make it complete. It is unfinished. The only thing that will complete that wall as a finished product is the brick—whatever size or shape it may be. Until then it is not complete. Loneliness is like that. Something is missing and so long as that something is missing, the "wall of our life" is incomplete. When there is emptiness in our life, there is loneliness. There is an incompleteness.

Loneliness is both negative and positive. Negative loneliness occurs when we are lonely, and we don't know what is missing in our lives. It is the loneliness of longing and feeling alone and empty. We feel a void, and the emptiness, but we cannot define or name what is missing. It is the loneliness of the unknown. It is felt deeply but we don't know what is causing the pain of loneliness. This feeling is a great part of teenage loneliness.

Another negative experience of loneliness happens when we feel a crushing loneliness and we know what is missing. We know what we need and want, but our need is not possible to meet. This is the loneliness of realizing that we can never recapture what we had. It is gone and it will never return. It cannot return. This is not the loneliness of death. It is the loneliness of life. What is gone is what we had in life. The persons are still there, and life goes on. What was a special relationship at one point in life will never be the same again. This may be the sorrow of divorce or broken relationships.

There is a positive element in loneliness, too. This is the loneliness that we feel when we miss a loved one who also misses us. Perhaps we are separated from one another by distance, by geography. We can explain this loneliness. We know why we are lonely. This loneliness, although deep, is a happy one because we know the source and extent of it. We know the reason for it. We know it is a loneliness that will be turned into joy when we are once again reunited with the person we miss so deeply. This is the loneliness of joyful longing and expectation. It is full of hope. Unlike the loneliness of the unrecoverable loss, this is the loneliness of temporary separation from the good we know and love.

Loneliness has a solution. That is to discover within ourselves a loneliness for the greatest good, God. We have reflected often that no self-created good can fill the longing within us for the ultimate eternal good. It is after having passed through the many experiences of the loneliness of life that we are able to understand why we are so vulnerable to loneliness and we are sensitive to this common experience. It is essential to our existence. We are finite creatures with the potential for perfect happiness. Until we have perfect happiness, we will always feel an emptiness and an aloneness.

The grace given to us by God is to know why loneliness is part of the fabric of our being. It is to know its meaning. Being lonely and knowing emptiness are not ends in themselves. It is to know that ultimately we long for God and that we seek him as the fulfillment of our aspirations. We will be lonely, but we will be able to embrace our loneliness and recognize it as a deep call from God. That holy moment of awareness will enable us to speak from our heart, "Lord, it is you whom my heart seeks."

27

Holiday
Loneliness

R ight after Thanksgiving, we enter officially into the
Christmas season with its decorations, high-pressured
sales, and advertising. The Sunday following Thanksgiving
is the beginning of the season of Advent.

History shows that the season of Advent is the most
tragic time of year with the most family tensions, family
breakups, and the time when there is a great increase in attempted suicides. It may become a time of financial stress
and a reminder of our personal financial limitations. This
can be a miserable time for the poor who, perhaps now more
than ever, are aware of how poor they are. They cannot buy
things, and society makes them objects of charity in its struggle to rid itself of the burden of having to look upon the sufferings of the poor. Often, for the more affluent, there is
a push and rush in trying to meet deadlines. December can
be a month of trying to get four weeks work done in three,
and of trying to appear happy doing it.

We sing, "Tis the season to be jolly, yet sometimes we
ask ourselves, "whom are we trying to kid?" Perhaps there
is nothing to be jolly about. We are apt to push ourselves
to the breaking point of physical and emotional fatigue in

shopping and partying. We may overspend in order to keep up with the Jones' in a tradition of giving that misses the whole point of giving. Then, after we reach the zenith of Christmas, we may be plunged into the crushing emptiness and loneliness that sometimes follows Christmas. It is an experience of emptiness and loneliness which may reoccur every year.

Why does all this happen? It happens because some strive and struggle to achieve happiness where it is not. They behave like dogs at the track chasing the rabbit. They chase, chase, and never catch it. What this reveals for some is our total immersion in materialism and commercialism. They have completely taken the spirituality out of Christmas so that when Christmas is past, they say, "Thank God, it is over for another year."

Maybe there is a good side to this loneliness. Perhaps there is something good that can come out of it. Loneliness is the absence of good. When we are lonely we lack a certain "good" in ourselves. It is not complete emptiness, but it is a certain emptiness that many times we cannot explain or describe. It is just there.

Loneliness is the reminder that when we are lonely, we are lonely for God — the only true "good" who can completely satisfy us. We can either make a mad dash to satisfy that loneliness through some activity, through some association, or by the possession of some material good. We might go so far as to try to lose loneliness in alcohol. But we find that none of these cures does lasting good. Loneliness either does not go away or it returns soon.

The other road we can take in loneliness is to slow down, be introspective, and let God speak to us as we listen in the silence and peace of contemplation. Loneliness is a call to comtemplation. We should not miss the call. It is a summons to listen to God and take our instructions from him in silence. It is in this silence that we allow God to fill us with his peace. We have missed God, and we are now letting God come to us.

Loneliness is a reminder that we are in a kind of exile. Loneliness tells us that we do not have a lasting city in this life. The older we get, the more we find ourselves beset by loneliness. This is natural with the ebbing of our physical strength and mental capabilities. The more funerals we attend, the more obituaries we read, the closer we are brought to the reality of our own death. It is not easy to contemplate death. Our increased loneliness through age is part of our dying process. It makes us homesick for our true home. "By the streams of Babylon we sat and wept when we remembered Zion." (Psalms 136)

For some, the Christmas rush accentuates the state of loneliness, emptiness, and frustration because of its materialism. Let them take the terrible loneliness resulting from the let-down and allow this loneliness to teach them to retreat into their consciousness and listen to God. Let this loneliness remind them that this life isn't their true lasting home. That home is somewhere else and it is much better. When looked at in this way, loneliness is not all bad. There is something good about it.

28

Spirituality in Many Guises

*A*fter the Protestant Reformation, the Roman Catholic Church had to buckle down to getting things in order within its own ranks. Because of the need to emphasize the presence of Jesus in the Most Blessed Sacrament of the Altar, the church building became a quiet tomb of solemnity and silence. The focal point was the tabernacle. It was beautiful. The church structure and all appointments centered on the adoration of the eucharist. When one entered the church, one was struck by the majesty of the presence of God, and the necessity of being prayerfully reverent.

After the Reformation, the Church placed less emphasis on devotion to the Holy Spirit, devotion to the Sacred Scriptures, and the importance of fellowship as part of Christian worship.

After Vatican II, these discarded elements were revived. Some thought this kind of revival signaled the downfall of the Church and the "Protestantizing" of the Catholic Church. Actually, it was the restoration of what had been before and what was needed now. Some received it with great joy. Acceptance depended on one's point of reference and on one's psychological leanings and attitudes.

Through the charismatic renewal, the Church responded by recapturing devotions neglected for a long time. Once again parishioners began to read the Scripture, invoke the Holy Spirit, and share with one another the joys of prayer and worship. This was good especially when believers throughout the world came to life in the joy of this emphasis. For years, we had neglected to fulfill the religious needs of many. People are not all the same, and their needs are different.

At the end of every millennium there is the psychological phenomenon of the "end of the world" anxiety. It happens every thousand years. It is natural. Anxiety takes the form of fundamentalism and rapturism. These views are around us now and appeal to a certain type of person. These outlooks are not theology. It is mass psychology. There are the fundamentalist thinkers and they must be cared for and ministered to. For a long time people who were not being fed by the silent contemplative church and its style of worship experienced a kind of religious starvation and left the Church.

One danger which must always be avoided in fundamentalism is the tendency to replace the Eucharist with the Word. This is one of the inherent weaknesses of fundamentalist thought. Also, there is the trend in some circles to make worship a kind of rock concert. Supposedly, the louder and more involved we become, the better the worship. A musician told me that rock groups played loudly so as to cover up how poorly they played. A nurse told me she was going to return to the Church and begin practicing her faith again. She said she was going to begin this return by attending the "way-out" parish because it did not make any spiritual demands. Recently I heard that one woman had said that if she wanted a "cultural" shock, she could attend a particular charismatic parish and the shock would take place. The shock would be experienced in the difference between the silent parish and the charismatic one. These points go together as we see how people react to the diversity of modes of worship. It is natural for many to see a "way-out" place as not very spiritual. Like it or not, that is the way such parishes are sometimes described. People see that parishes and prayer styles are different, and they classify them.

On the other hand, we have the contemplative and solemn worship style of parish and person. "In our parish, Father has it down to such a prayerful atmosphere." This kind of person likes what is happening and has found a style of worship that is satisfying. There are people who link worship with silence together with a contemplative style that bespeaks profound reverence. It is the individual who makes the generalization. This kind of religious expression can be a real "drag" for some, especially the young.

In a parish untouched by Vatican II people are likely to object to any changes in the Church. They are not charismatics, fundamentalists, or contemplatives. They are traditional Roman Catholics. Their devotion consists in preserving the past.

These examples support the point of these reflections. We follow our psychological bent. If we have a charismatic leaning, we will be Charismatics. We will go where we will be fed. In religious expression, as in food and music, there are differences. It would be funny to have the ticket-takers at a large cultural center get their stations mixed up and send the patrons of the acid rock concert into the auditorium where *Lohengrin* was being performed. With the diversity of worship, we will likewise seek the one that is natural to our temperament.

We will find few mystics in the charismatic movement and few fundamentalists among the contemplatives. These are two very different modes of religious expression. They appeal to people according to the makeup and temperament of each person. For many years, we were expected to be in one mold. Now, people of the same household—well-intentioned and spiritual—claim their own form of spirituality. A wife may be a charismatic; the husband may be contemplative. One family member may be a fundamentalist who quotes the Bible all day long yet does not affect the rest of the family. It may not always make for the greatest harmony, but now that there are many ways open to us, we will follow the way that is most natural, most suited to our personality, and most personally fulfilling.

We have to be accepting of each other. We cannot insult or make fun of another. Such attitudes are not spirituality. For example, those of us who have not gone into the charismatic form of worship are not to ridicule that religious expression. Our psychology may lead us to a definite form of worship, but our charity will accept all forms of religious expression. We invite all the children of God to come together around his holy table.

29

Catholics
The Sadducees

*T*he Pharisees of biblical times believed in salvation through the Law. The conversion of Paul was not conversion to the belief that Jesus had risen from the dead. That was no problem for Paul nor for any other Pharisee. As Pharisees, they believed the resurrection was essential to their belief. They believed in resurrection and eternal life, but that resurrection came through observance of the Law. Paul's conversion was from belief that salvation comes through the Law to a belief in salvation through Christ. The Pharisees were a pious, rigid group that did not waver in their practice of the Mosaic Law. By the time the Gospels were written they had come to take quite a beating and we have a dismal picture of Phariseeism.

The Sadducees denied the resurrection. They were a religious group within Judaism but since they did not believe in the resurrection nor in life eternal, the motions of religion that they practiced were empty rituals.

Protestants are called "Modern Day Pharisees" because of their strict disciplines toward church attendance, abstentions, and adherence to the prescriptions of the written word. Heaven is for the good and for those who hear the word of the Lord and who put it into practice.

Catholics are called the "Modern Day Sadducees" because of the number of rituals that had crept into Catholic devotion through the ages and had perdured and been part of the upbringing of many. We had come to the point where we practiced certain rituals without knowing what they meant, where they came from, nor why we went through the rituals.

When the French and Germans took control of the liturgy in the middle ages and as the Arian and Jansenistic persuasions made their influence in worship, the concept of God and prayer reflected the unworthiness of the human person before the awesome presence of God. The altar was moved far away. The people were separated from the priest by a communion railing, and the priest celebrated the Mass in silence and in an unknown tongue with his back to the people. The only clue to what was going on was a bell rung by the server. In fact, the bell came to have such importance that some thought that without the bell, there was no consecration. This opened the door for private devotions during the Mass and for a heavy concentration on pious ritual. Breast-beating at the Sanctus, at the consecration, and at the Agnus Dei came into vogue. The sacramentals took on new importance. Holy water, blessed palms, and especially, ashes assumed a place in Catholic devotion that superseded the eucharist.

Then came Vatican II, and the modern day Sadducees stood up to be counted. I found that when the original changes in the liturgy first came about, some of the priests could not make an intelligent change or give a good explanation because their own understanding of why we had done certain things was lacking. Mass continued in Latin and their lack of knowledge of what they were saying in Latin was a drawback.

Such changes hit the people hard. They objected when the altar was turned around and the communion railing removed. They objected when the liturgy was said in English and when the explanations for the use of the holy water and the triple sign of the cross at the Gospel were given. When given the reason that the priest did not conduct the liturgy of the Word from behind the altar people resisted. The changes evoked sharp responses. "I don't like it! That is not the way I was taught." When they were asked for reasons for many of their reactions, people could not give reasons except that "That was the way they were taught by the Sisters in grade school back in Chicago or Philadelphia ... " This was clearly a case of Saduceeism. Practices and rituals were performed without reason and without meaning.

We clergy did not do much to help our people. We initiated many changes abruptly and without sufficient explanation, and as a result we did offend. I have to take considerable blame for this suffering because I was too hurried, and I forgot that others didn't know what I was thinking. But now, we are actually less Sadducee than we were before Vatican II. Now we have a better idea of what we are doing and why.

30

Blessed
Are the Meek

*I*n the great Broadway musical, *Camelot,* King Arthur's
illegitimate son, Mordred, sings an amusing number
blaspheming the Sermon on the Mount. In the song he refers
to the meek as those who inherit – not the earth – but the
dirt. He is not far from wrong. Who are the ones who get
the dirt? They are the meek and humble of heart. People
walk on the meek, and seem to push them around because
the meek have control of their anger. Such control reflects
great inner strength. In fact, it is the weak who cannot show
meekness and who rely on the strength of the meek when
they, the weak, manifest their own lack of personal self-
assurance and their own sense of failure. It is not the meek
who promote their strong points. It is not the meek who bul-
ly others in venting their personal frustrations. Meekness
is the strength of truth and reality that can respond to others
who cry out in their deep-seated frustrations.

Meekness is closely associated with a humility that
does not get disturbed nor agitated over the latest fad, trend,
movement. Such meekness is not impressed by the hard-
pressure salesperson who has the "latest and best thing going." Meekness calmly relates and compassionately responds
to people and situations as they are.

The definition and description of meekness is the controlling of one's anger in the present situation – to respond in love to what is happening. It is realizing what people are telling us when they are angry. When others scream at us and tell us off, and tell us how much better they are, then true meekness is operative. Angry people show how much they are hurting and where they are hurting. They tell us that they are suffering grievously. Meekness is the ability to allow persons to suffer pain and to accept them in their suffering without letting ourselves increase that suffering. Meekness is the grace of God that allows the frustrated to express suffering even though the object of such expression might be ourselves. Meekness resists the temptation to rejoice in the sufferings of those who cause us pain.

On the contrary, meekness enters and suffers doubly. The meek suffer when another person vents frustration and sorrow. It is never easy to take the wrath of another even though that wrath is not inspired by hatred. We suffer when there is no solution to the situation except patient suffering and time. The meek person does not gloat at the agony of another, but rather suffers with and suffers for.

In such suffering and in such acceptance, a meek person might, as Mordred says, "inherit the dirt." However, a person possessing the quality of meekness has a self-possession, a serenity, a calmness, and a peace that holds within it the seed of Jesus' promise, "Blessed are the meek. They shall inherit the earth."

31

Jealousy and Envy

*I*n his first letter to the people of Corinth, the Apostle Paul writes, "Let there be no factions." This is a good admonition. In every group and organization there will be factions, divisions, and splits. This happens because not everyone will occupy the same position of authority or control. There is something else we must all face. Not everyone has the same ability, talent, and intelligence. These differences are difficult in some circles. When I was a young priest I heard, "Ability be damned. We are all the same." Fellow priests did not believe these statements and neither did I, but it was a necessary lie that allowed imcompetents who could never make it otherwise a place of respect. Because there are marked individual differences in talent, ability, and intelligence, some will occupy posts of greater importance in any society. That is the way it has to be. For that reason there will be jealousy and envy. This is particularly devastating when we find jealousy and envy in persons of authority.

Jealousy in our lives can be measured by our criticism of those around us, or even of those we don't know. Criticism reflects failure to admit the good that others have. One of the greatest sufferings of Jesus was that he had to contend with the refusals of his enemies to see the good in what he was doing. His patience was most tried when they ascribed his works of healing to the evil one. He called this the sin against the Holy Spirit.

We can recall some examples in our experience and see why we might not like a person, but we must give that person credit for the good he is doing or for the talent he possesses. Muhammed Ali is a controversial figure. There are many people who do not like him, because of his style and personality. But who can deny his ability as a boxer? Where good is, there must be recognition of that good. John McEnroe may not be the most popular athlete, but he can play tennis. Everyone must admit that.

There are three sins that jealousy and envy produce. The first is the sin of failing to see the good wherever it may be. It is the refusal to acknowledge that there is good and that a certain person does have ability, talent, and intelligence apart from what we personally might think of this person. In the movie *Keys of the Kingdom* when the town is under attack, Father Chisolm tells the mother superior "We must put aside our personal differences now."

The second sin, produced by jealousy and envy, occurs when we put on the brakes and stop progress because we are not capable of effecting that progress. This is especially true if we are in charge. If we are in command and find that subordinates are more capable and more energetic, it is a common escape mechanism to slow a whole process down, or to stop it entirely. We neither do anything nor allow anything to be done. If we are creative, that is all right. If we are not creative and do not allow creative persons the freedom to work, then it is not all right. It is a sin and it is serious.

The third, and perhaps the most insidious of these sins, is to let our jealousy and our envy show by building up those persons who have neither talent nor ability. It is a crushing burden to listen while a dullard is praised for talents he does not have. He is not praised for his talents. We praise and build up dullards and "dead wood" even though we know there is no truth in what we say. Such an approach gives vent to the jealousy of a trouble maker who sees a golden opportunity to create some discord.

An example may prove the point: If an outfielder drops every flyball hit to him, and if he strikes out everytime he gets up to bat, we don't storm the office demanding he be declared MVP. That can create much hardship and suffering. It is jealousy at its height.

What do we do about jealousy and envy? Once again we face the question of "letting go," a characteristic of Christianity and descriptive of it. We must let go. It is in letting go or in the daily dying that we accomplish this. We must die to ourselves in loving God and others. In this dying to self, we die to our jealousy and to our envy.

32
Worship of Evil

A most distressing development following the rise of the popularity of prayer groups is the emphasis placed on the devil and evil. I say it is distressing because when people gather to pray, to praise God, adore his mercy, and celebrate his forgiveness—what do they hear?—a lot of devil talk. Often, more attention and time are given to the devil and to the powers of evil than to God and to his redeeming love. It disturbs me to see and hear people reverse the roles and give the devil so much attention.

Recently, I read a treatise written by a prominent leader of prayer groups. The devil seemed to have been mentioned on every page at least five times. There was emphasis on the inroads and successes the devil was making. The essay was intended to be about spirituality and prayer, not a paper on demonology. In a conversation I had with the author of this paper, she informed me that all illness comes from the devil. The results of this kind of thinking are quite clear. When these people pray for healing, they condemn the sick person as being wicked or in league with evil powers. If there is no immediate healing, then that person has chosen to remain in union with those powers. That is an alarming attitude and is harmful.

Sister Helen—beautiful, capable, saintly—died of

cancer. During the two years of illness prior to her death, everyone was affected and concerned. On one occasion, an individual prayed over her and almost frightened her to death by screaming, "TUMOR, LEAVE THIS BODY AND GO BACK TO HELL WHERE YOU CAME FROM." Sister never did believe that her lymphoma came from hell. The suggestion that it came from hell did little to help her.

A sincere, dedicated couple reported this experience: One night they awakened and were aware of the presence of evil around them. That sort of thing is outlandish. People who live in the state of grace, who pray, and who act according to the command of Jesus to love God and neighbor have no need to fear the presence of the devil in their house.

A well-known Catholic magazine stated that the sign of the presence of the devil in the world today is the way nuns have discarded the religious habit. Is this not a ridiculous judgment? The religious garb was originally the dress worn by the women of the day, especially by widows. Then it became a religious custom to dress virgins in the garb of these non-virgins. If we were to turn that statement around, we could say that the sign of the presence of God in the world is the dressing of virgins in the costume of non-virgins. If religious women are not a witness to the world of their dedication by their lives, then yards of wool will not do it.

At issue is an atmosphere of devil-worship and evil-worship. We appear to be more concerned with the devil than with God – more with sin than with grace – more with hell than with heaven. What are we all about, and what are we supposed to be doing? What are we supposed to be talking about? We are called to bring to the minds of all that we are unconditionally loved by a God who loves us more than we can imagine. We have been redeemed by Jesus who showed the extent and depth of his love by giving his life for us on the cross.

In response to the last temptation in the desert when the evil one asked Jesus to bow down and worship him, Jesus said, "Begone, Satan, the Lord your God will you adore and him alone shall you serve." This is also our best attitude. Let us worship God and adore him. Let us believe evil is overcome by love, and know again that love casts out all fear.

33

Christmas
A Love Story

*T*he children's liturgy was filled with the pageantry of the Nativity. There were shepherds and angels and everything else that make the Christmas Eve Mass beautiful and meaningful for children and parents, as well as for the liturgist and the pastor. What made this liturgy unique was that a young girl dressed like Blessed Mother held a newborn baby boy. That baby enabled us to realize that we were witnessing the true meaning of Christmas. Christmas is a story of a birth.

The analogy was brought to us that this teen-age girl, holding a baby, was what happened in Bethlehem when Mary, a teen-age girl, held her infant son.

Something wonderful happened in the church at that moment. We were transformed into people in love. All it takes to soften our hearts, to slow us down to experience new life and new hope, is a baby. There is something about a baby that is basic to us and we respond in a most tender way. We found that we were in love. We were in love with a new life before us. We were drawn by that love to the young girl and to the baby she was holding. We found ourselves closer to one another as we shared the same experience.

Christmas is a love story. It is the story of God the Father who fell in love with a beautiful Jewish girl and who chose her to be the instrument of the revelation of the Incarnation. One of the most tender of loves is the love of mother for her infant. This is the reason God the Father chose to reveal the mystery of the redemption by means of a birth. God the Son was born of a beautiful Jewish girl. In this tender love of mother for her infant, we closely approach the love of God for us.

Another love that closely resembles the love of God is the love of mother. It has been said that the love of God the Father for us is the love of God the Mother. The love of a mother is an engulfing love. The love of mother is the love of one who is in love.

For us to grasp the beauty and meaning of Christmas, we must fall in love. If Christmas is the story of the falling in love of God with us, if Christmas is the story of the falling in love of God with Mary, if Christmas is the story of the falling in love of Mary with her son, then we will but stand on the periphery of the total picture and be distant onlookers unless we ourselves fall in love. We must fall in love with Jesus and Mary and with each other; then we will fall in love with God the Father.

When we are in love, everything looks wonderful, bright, and rosy. Everybody seems to be our friend and beautiful. We speak in a silly way, and act in a silly manner, and others ask, "What's with them?" and the answer comes back, "Oh, they're in love. Can't you tell?" What a delight to see couples in love; what a delight when we are in love.

Isn't it significant that the coming of the Prince of Peace is a love story? Isn't it remarkable that peace and love go together? Peace will reign in the hearts of those who love and who bring love to others. Christmas is a love story and peace is a love story. These two love stories are the keys to our own life. We must love in order to have peace, but we really don't know love until we fall in love. We must fall in love. God did, why can't we?

34

Desecration
of the Eucharist

W hen the question of communion in the hand and communion of both species was first raised, there was
furor in some churches about so-called desecration of the
eucharist or the Sacred Species. This was even written by
people who claimed the title, theologian. But it was a play
upon the feelings of the unlearned and the unsuspecting
under the guise of respect. It was actually a push for false
piety to lay a "heavy trip" on the pious and the humble in
order to prevent movement and progress in liturgy. It was
almost total manipulation that victimized those who held
a strong devotion to the eucharist.

The argument centered on the spilling of the precious
blood and the delay in the consuming of the sacred host
by communion in the hand. These arguments made no real
sense, but they did serve to disturb the innocent and the
unsuspecting. It was an attempt to sacralize species. But the
reason for it exemplified desecration more than anything
else. This is because when we sacralize, we tend to desecrate
the real meaning of what the eucharist and the other
sacraments are all about.

Jesus, the God of all sanctity, was born in a stable,

surrounded by animals and the dung of those animals. There was no desecration there because straw, dung, and dirt are part of God's creation of our world. Had the question of desecration been present, God would have had Jesus born in an airtight bubble to make sure his flesh never touched anything common. There was the Immaculate Conception but not the antiseptic birth.

Jesus walked the streets of Nazareth, Capernaum, and Jerusalem with dirty feet, matted hair, and body odor. Very likely he had bad breath, too. But in all this, there was no desecration of his sacred person: his body odor and bad breath did not desecrate anyone. On the other hand, there was desecration when James and John demanded to be given top honors. There was desecration when his enemies tried to trap Jesus in his speech. There was desecration when he was struck after giving an answer to the high priest. There was desecration when he was whipped, pushed, mocked, and finally crucified. I prefer to think that there was no desecration when he was pierced with a lance. What is done through pride, malice, and cruelty constitutes desecration. When there is no pride, malice, nor cruelty involved, there is no desecration.

Probably one of the cruelest things I can think of is to sit at table to eat and then deny someone a place at that table, or deny someone food. This just screams to me as utmost cruelty. This is desecration of a person. When we treat a person this cruelly, there is a real desecration. And this is also the desecration of Jesus and the desecration of the eucharist. The sharing of a meal is a basic act of community living and worship. When we deny a person a place at that table or when we make another person so miserable that he loses all desire to eat or to share, then we are guilty of a crime that cries to heaven for vengeance.

Our hatred, malice, and lack of acceptance of others are acts of the desecration of the eucharist today. If we approach the communion table in a state of enmity and isolation, this is desecration. It is hard to see how we can claim eucharist when we have a church filled with people who are there physically, but who are not present to each other. It is like sitting down to dinner where no one speaks. This is simply ingestion of food. This is what amoebae and paramecia do. They don't have dinner, they ingest. When we feed the cat, that cat purrs and is aware of the presence of the owner who feeds it. When two people sit down at table either at home or a restaurant and don't communicate, but just ingest, that is desecration. It is taking the sacred moments of mealtime and destroying the time by the lack of sharing. When people enter the church building and go through the motions of worship, but are not present to each other, and when the priest stands at the altar offering the sacred mysteries and is not present to the people, there is desecration.

Worse is when people receive communion and continue to harbor hatred and anger toward their neighbor, come into the same temple and ignore one another, and then leave the temple without speaking to one another. We then have the worst form of desecration of the eucharist.

If a particle of the host falls to the ground and some of the precious blood is spilled on the carpet, there is no desecration. When people partake of the body and the blood of Jesus with closed hearts, then there is great desecration.

35
Union of Wills

"O Jesus, Eternal High Priest, I unite my entire will with yours this day, in my prayer, works, sufferings, and joys." This is like many other offerings we make in the morning and renew often during the day. Through this type of dedication, we place ourselves at the disposal of Our Blessed Lord, and we place our wills in union with his.

As we renew the act of union, we live by actual intention and go beyond the virtual intention. Virtual intention means that we make our intention to live in union with Jesus throughout our day. We never retract intention because we mean it. But we make it once and then never renew it. It is like putting on your aftershave in the morning, and leaving it on all day. Intention is good, necessary, and praiseworthy, but really it does not go far enough.

Actual intention is one whereby we make our act of union and never take it back, and keep on sincerely making over and over again all during our day as the circumstances of our day change and progress. This is the intention of sanctity. If we want to be saints, then let us live by actual intention.

The actual intention of union with the will of Jesus is based on his sacred humanity. Jesus, as son of God, is the redeemer of the world who by his death on the cross pays to his Eternal Father the price of our salvation. Because he is God, he can pay the infinite price. But Jesus is also man – perfect man. He is the son of many. As son of many – as perfect man – he wins for us all the actual graces that we need in our day-by-day journey to the Father. "No one comes to the Father except through me."

The goal of every person is to come to the Father. Jesus reminds us that only through him will we achieve this goal. When we join with Jesus in his sacred humanity in the varied events of our lives, we receive from him the graces to live our life following in his footsteps. We allow his sacred huminity to be more than an example for us. Actually, we allow his sacred humanity to be the strength and the grace of our life at this moment and in this circumstance.

If I am frustrated in my work plans, then I merely look to Jesus in his sacred humanity – many times frustrated – and join my will with his. "Jesus, you took many frustrations, you know all about them. I unite my will with yours now in this one I have to take." As we grow more accustomed to this, it becomes increasingly a part of our every moment, thought, and intention. We do it with a glance. This then applies to everything we do. If we are eating, sleeping, playing, praying, working, driving, or flying in a jet aircraft, it is all the same.

We know much more about the physical sciences today than Jesus knew, but he knows about all the sciences in us. Jesus lives in us, prays in us, works in us, and plays in us. Jesus is the eternal adorer of his Heavenly Father, and he adores the Father in us and through us. So when we turn on our TV sets, Jesus in his sacred humanity adores the Father. And when we watch television or drive our late-model car equipped with stereo and air conditioning, we unite our wills to that of Jesus in our travel, work, and enjoyment. And Jesus adores the Eternal Father in the progress of humanity in science, learning, and development. Jesus lives in us today and he adores the Father in us and through us.

Jesus tells us that he always does the things that please the Father. Here is where our union with him, in his sacred humanity, comes through for us. We unite our wills with his and join in his eternal adoration. And we receive the actual graces for this moment.

If we are in a state of suffering – like the suffering of a severe sorrow – then we make our union with Jesus who said, "My soul is sorrowful even unto death." Immediately, we receive from him the grace to live with this sorrow as he lived with his. But when we unite our wills with that of Jesus in this sorrow, he does not take the sorrow away. When we unite our wills with that of Jesus in joy or in success, we do not expect him to take away that joy or that success. We receive the grace to live with it and not to waste the moment of grace in sorrow or in joy or whatever.

This is what Jesus means when he says, "Apart from me you can do nothing." There will be a terrible waste of our life and effort without this union. And because of our human weakness, and our failure to maintain this union, there will be a three-step procedure that we will have to follow repeatedly all our life.

First, is the contrition for our sin. We had made the intention of this act of union, and had broken it by our own contrary will. So we make an act of contrition expressing our sorrow. "O God, my God, forgive me for my deliberate failure to keep my promise to you."

Second, comes the act of humility. This acknowledges our total dependence upon the mercy of God. This is the necessary element for any spiritual growth. Without humility we are without a base. God resists the proud, but gives his grace to the humble.

Finally, comes the renewed act of union as we unite our will to that of Jesus, not because we deserve it nor because we are good, but because he is good and we need. As we endeavor to do the will of the Father, we unite our will with that of Jesus who does the will of his Father.

36

In My Name

*I*n the farewell discourses of Jesus, we find in the Gospel of John that Our Blessed Lord makes the statement to his disciples, "Until now you have not asked for anything in my name. Ask and you will receive and your joy will be complete." These words of consolation and comfort prompt us to inquire, "What does it mean to ask in the name of Jesus?"

We end so many of our prayers with "Through Christ Our Lord." This does not mean that we are praying in his name. This is merely a beautiful conclusion. We can remain in our own self-will, love, and selfishness and say . . . "through Christ Our Lord" all day long and it will remain just an empty meaningless expression. To pray in Christ's name goes far beyond the words we utter. It is the spirit that gives life; whereas, the words kill.

When Our Blessed Lord told the apostles that up to that time they had not prayed in his name, he was not scolding them nor degrading them. At that time, the meaning of the life and death of Jesus had not been revealed to them. They did not understand that the Messiah had to suffer and die in obedience to his Father's will. They had not seen the capture, passion, and death of Jesus; they had yet to witness the resurrection. Without this knowledge, they could not possibly pray in his name because the meaning of his name had not been manifest.

To pray in the name of Jesus is to return to the letter to the Philippians and to examine the Philippian hymn (2:5-11). Paul tells the people of Philippi that their minds must be the mind of Christ, who though he was God did not grasp what was rightly his. He emptied himself and became obedient for us unto death – even death on a cross. Then God exalted him and gave him a name above every other name. At the name of Jesus every knee shall bend.

To pray in the name of Jesus is to assume the same attitude and thought of Jesus who emptied himself. To pray in the name of Jesus is to empty ourselves with the very giving over of self to God and to his mercy and providence. When we can adopt the mind-set of Jesus and be totally open to God and submissive to his will in our lives, then, and then alone, will we pray in the name of Jesus. Then we will ask, receive, and our joy will be complete.

37

Holy Mary

*I*n the great Wagnerian opera, *Tannhauser*, the sad hero, Tannhauser, wishes to be freed from the spell of Venus and released from the sensual paradise, Venusberg, and return to earth. Venus ridicules Tannhauser for such a wish and tells him that he is doomed. He will not be accepted by his people and, most of all, he will not find forgiveness from his Christian God. With a vociferous cry, Tannhauser proclaims to Venus that he places his hope in the Virgin Mary. At the sound of the name of the Blessed Virgin, the spell is broken. Venus shrieks and disappears. At the end of the opera when the Pilgrims return from Rome, showing that Tannhauser has received forgiveness from God, the impact of this first scene is revived. He had placed his hope in the Blessed Virgin Mary, and in the end, against all odds and obstacles, receives forgiveness and salvation. It is all beauty.

Tannhauser is only a legend, but there is something similar going on today when, at the mention of the name of Mary, the Venuses of today cry out, retreat, and disappear. As Venus could not stand the sound of the name of the Blessed Virgin Mary, there are many today who will not tolerate her, and will almost clap their hands over their ears in order not to hear her name. But as in the legend of Tannhauser, it is in that name that the spell will be broken.

At the time of the Protestant reformation, the teachings of the Reformers emphasized the person of Jesus as the only mediator between God and man. This weakened the doctrine of the communion of saints, and it also brought in the human element of not allowing anyone else in one's relationship to God. Eventual pitfalls were spiritual pride and jealousy. Much of the antagonism to Blessed Mother is rooted in jealousy. Why does she receive that honor? Who is she? Spiritual jealousy is no small matter because if we fall prey to it, we can become hardened, unbending, and unmerciful.

Closely associated with this was the natural problem of what happens when you take away the female element from devotion and worship. God created male and female; to survive we need both. Within every human there are both male and female elements. The woman carries the man, and we call this the animus. The man carries a woman with him, and we call this the anima. In the case of the man, the anima tempers his masculine traits with softness and gentleness. The anima is associated always with the mother's love.

The female is necessary for our completeness. When the Reformers took the female element from devotion and worship, they lost an essential and necessary part of human need. They then produced a stone God—totally masculine—with little mercy or compassion. Humans need the two elements, and they had these two in the eucharist—the humanity of Christ, and the devotion to Blessed Mother. Without them, we had imbalance in our devotional life. One of the results was the severe, stern punishing God of the Puritans. It was a psychological loss, but it was also a spiritual loss.

The Catholic Church, in order to preserve the sanctity of the Most Blessed Sacrament, emphasized the real presence and made the church building a silent tomb of solemn worship before the awesome presence of God. There was no talking and no noise. The liturgy was prayed in silence, and the people became onlookers of a drama called the Mass. Three important elements, proper to the church, were dropped from their place of prominence. These were 1) the devotion to the Holy Spirit, 2) the devotion to the Sacred Scriptures, and 3) the aspect of fellowship so necessary to Christian community. During this time, the devotion to the eucharist was stressed as being thoroughly Catholic, and with it grew the devotion to the Mother of God. When we emphasize the humanity of Christ, we naturally bring in the mother. Through the ages up to the time of Vatican II, the eucharist and the Marian devotion were associated with Catholicism. Protestantism was known more for the use of the sacred word and for Christian fellowship.

Vatican II did much to upset this stereotype. The Catholic Church embraced the charismatic movement, and devotion to the Holy Spirit was revived together with the renewed enthusiasm for the sacred scriptures. There was a new pentecost as the church branched out and was enabled to be open and appeal to people of different temperaments and needs. But this had its perils. It was like opening the floodgates to the enthusiastic and the unlearned of which St. Peter spoke. In many ways, Vatican II appealed to people who, like students who had had a rough semester and had barely made it, were given another chance with a new course the next semester. However, in the enthusiastic pursuit for the word and the holy spirit, there were many who lost their devotion to the blessed eucharist and the blessed mother.

There was a form of the Docetist heresy that entered into the church and spread mistrust of all humanity, including the humanity of Christ. But if we deny the humanity of Jesus, we deny that he was born of a woman; and eventually, we will repudiate the eucharist, declaring that for our spiritual growth all we need is the word and the spirit. The denial of the eucharist is the modern-day Docetism that says, "Everything is spiritual—there is nothing visible and tangible and the word did not become flesh but only word." Docetism attacks both Jesus and Mary, his mother, in the eucharist.

But look at what happens, humanly speaking, when we forego the humanity of Christ and the devotion to the mother of Jesus. We lose the tenderness of motherhood and the softness of womanhood. And we also lose the respect for woman. It is this sort of thinking that has brought on the increased incidents of rape and attempted rape and other forms of violence against women and children. Look at places like El Salvador where children are tortured, or Iran, where mothers are tortured in front of their children. It is a sick global system. But global violence is the reflection of individual violence. And our individual violence is the result of our loss of the spirit of gentleness that is both proper in women and to the respect of women. This disrespect is directly traceable to the withdrawal from devotion to the Mother of God—a devotion that reminds us of the gentleness of God's love.

In addition to the effect repudiation of womanhood and of the blessed mother has had on our civil and religious society, there is something that has happened to us spiritually as well. This is the absence of those qualities that God taught us in the sacred scriptures about Mary, the blessed virgin. These are humilty, docility, and faith. Today, our feeble attempts at spirituality lack all three. Let us review them to see how, in blessed mother, they were fulfilled and why we need those same qualities now.

Humility—In the Magnificat, Mary proclaims the greatness of the Lord who has looked upon the humility of his handmaiden. God looked upon Mary in her humility. Humility is reality—knowing ourselves to be who we are before God. It is humility that is lacking in the spirituality of today, and in the charismatic groups that claim to have found God and been filled with the Holy Spirit. Instead of humility, there is pride, exclusiveness, and spiritual snobbery. Today the church, in so many of its forms, reeks of pride. Humility is replaced with canon law and literal fundamentalism, and bumper stickers that boast of a following of Christ rather than showing it by one's life. Who can claim with Blessed Mother, "The Lord has regarded my humility and he who is mighty has done great things for me"? If there is one definite characteristic of those who oppose blessed mother and decry the Marian devotion, it is the lack of humility.

Docility – At the Annunciation, Mary says, "Let it be done to me according to your word." The act of total submission to God, and the act of allowing him the freedom to work in her, and to accomplish his will in her will always distinguish her from us. This was different from the attitude of Zachary who doubted, argued, and resisted the action of God. Zachary had too much going for him intellectually and spiritually. He was not going to cooperate with the plan of God. He was building his own tower of Babel. In contrast, Blessed Mother, without understanding all the intricacies and details of God's will (we don't either, but at least she admitted it), gives her entire will over to that of God. There are so many Zacharys in the world and in the church today. Everyone is an expert on "what the Lord is doing and saying." What the world needs is fewer experts who seek to reveal the secrets of God, fewer interpreters of his will for others, and more people who can accept that will in their lives. But there is only one Blessed Mother.

Faith – At the visitation, Elizabeth speaks out about Mary, "Blessed is she who has believed." Humility, docility, and faith are sisters. They walk together. The proud person is low in faith, and the proud person is unteachable. The humility and docility of blessed mother are shown as the results of God's gift of faith to her. Faith is a gift of God to us and it was also a gift to Mary. Mary was able to take that step into the darkness and to live by faith because God bestowed the gift of a living, vibrant faith upon her. The reason she was declared blessed by Elizabeth was that she was not like Zachary who had too many reasons not to accept; she was not like Thomas who demanded to see the wounds; and she was not like our "enlightened" people of today who insist on seeing the chapter and verse.

Our world today is a faithless world filled with bitterness and pride. Today, so-called spirituality seeks to find God by its own activity, to put him in a neat little package, thereby avoiding the risk to believe anything. We live in an environment of contentions, jealousies, competition, and violence and other negatives that the Apostle Paul describes as the works of the flesh. And to top it off, we pass these off as spirituality. For these reasons, the world and the church will recoil at the thought of humility, docility, and faith. By the same token, the world will clap its hands over its ears so as not to hear the name of the one who exemplifies the three qualities: humility, docility, faith.

We live in a messed-up world. It is filled with hypocrisy and cruelty. We stand in need of the restoration of mercy, gentleness, and love. We live in a "Venusberg" of our own making. What can we do about it? I respond with the words of Tannhauser, "I put my hope in the Blessed Virgin Mary."